The Pen God Gave Me:

The Diary of My Soul

Ardreana Thompson

The Pen God Gave Me: The Diary of My Soul
Poems by: Ardreana Thompson

Cover by: Jazzy Kitty Publishing
Designed by: Jazzy Kitty Publishing
Logo Designs by: Andre M. Saunders/Leroy Grayson
Editor: Anelda L. Attaway

© 2013 Ardreana Thompson
ISBN 978-0-9892656-1-4
Library of Congress Control Number: 2013937444

All rights reserved. This book is protected under the copyright laws of the United States of America. No part of this publication may be reproduced or transmitted in any format or by any means electronic, mechanical, or otherwise, including photocopying, recording or any other storage or retrieval system without written permission of the publisher, except in the case of brief quotations embodied in critical articles or reviews.

For Worldwide Distribution. Printed in the United States of America. Published by Jazzy Kitty Greetings Marketing & Publishing, LLC. Utilizing Microsoft and Adobe Publishing Software. Utilizing Adobe and Microsoft Publishing Software.

ACKNOWLEDGMENTS

I would like to thank God for giving me the many people who have helped to make this lifelong dream come true.

To the entire Shoemaker/Thompson family: My Parents-Carl Thompson Sr. and the Late Dora Teresa (Shoemaker) Thompson for giving birth to me and raising me to be the beautiful Black rose that I have bloomed into; Thanks Mom and Dad! Also, I would like to thank my stepmother, Nora Thompson.

My six siblings for loving and nurturing me as their baby sister: The Late Linda Denise Shoemaker, Aaron Travell *(Bookie)* Shoemaker, Carl *(Big C)* Thompson Jr., Jeffrey, Charles, and Michael Thompson.

Those special members of my family *(The Shoemakers)* who never fail to give me that extra push: Deairra Shanie, Darrell Tolbert Jr., Arriel, Arryn, Donshic Shantel, Tandra Lashay, Tabitha Shareese, and Rafeal.

My best friend Tiffany Chevone Hartley: You have been there for me through it all. Thank you!

My pen sister, Jameese K. Wright: Thanks for believing that I could do it; you are indeed my pen twin.

To Sable Black: Thanks for everything and for being a friend.

Those who watched over me during the death of my mother.

To the most encouraging teacher that I have ever had, Mrs. Brenda Autry.

To Mr. Mike Guinn for guiding me through this road trip of finding myself as an author.

Last and not least, to Anelda Attaway of Jazzy Kitty Publishing for all of your guidance and support. You are a true blessing to my life, thank you for making my dream of a published author come true.

My ultimate goal was to believe in myself. I'm so glad that it didn't take this publication to achieve it. When I was at the lowest point of my life, it was friends and family who gave me something to believe in and that something is love. Once I learned to believe in love, I learned to believe in me.

DEDICATIONS

This book is dedicated to my stars in the sky!

The Late Dora Teresa (Shoemaker) Thompson

A.K.A.

Mom

And

The Late Linda Denise Shoemaker

A.K.A.

Big Sis

TABLE OF CONTENTS

Introduction *(Featured Poem: Even a Monster Cries)*	i
Entry I: Dear Diary/The Story Behind My Life	**01**
The Story Behind My Life	02
I'm A Woman	04
Stereotype of a Black Woman	07
Strength	09
My Identity	12
The Words I Write	15
Follow Your Dreams	17
Giving All But Me	21
Daydream	22
Inner self	25
Blood Type: Poetry	27
Entry II: Dear Diary/The Media	**28**
The Media	29
Even a Monster Cries	32
When	37
Devils	39
Confessions of Dirty Money *(Part I)*	42
Confessions of Dirty Money *(Part II)*	46
How a Crack Head is Made	49
How Do You Stop a Heart from Bleeding?	55

TABLE OF CONTENTS

Neka's Song	57
Baby	60
Being Black	62
New Found Respect	64
History	66
Where have all the Black Men Gone?	68
Enslaved Minds	70
A Child Worth Crying For	71
Take the Time	73
Dead Messenger	75
Entry III: Dear Diary/Beauty	**76**
Beauty	77
Blessed be the Man who Finds a Woman Like Me	81
Beautiful Thick Sista	83
My Sister	85
Stripes	86
Who I Am	89
I'm Trying to Do Me	91
The Price	93
Independent	95
Capture the Moment	98
The Embrace of Beauty	100

TABLE OF CONTENTS

I Could Never Deny the Fact 102
I Know What Love Is 104
Different 106
Making Me Happy 108
Love for Me 109
Entry IV: Dear Diary/The Faded Story (Then) 110
Entry IV: Dear Diary/The Faded Story (Now) 111
The Faded Story 112
Misery 121
If Only 124
She Screams 127
Road Trip 130
The Letter of a Scared Young Women 133
Tired of Living 135
Am I? 138
Finding a Way 140
Misunderstood 141
Memories 142
Beyond Recognition *(In My Trying Days)* 144
Entry V: Dear Diary/Finally 147
Things that only Came Once 149
Losing Mother 151

TABLE OF CONTENTS

Picture This	154
Emotional Questions	157
A Motherless Child	160
You Won't Let Me Cry	163
Set Your Heart on Heaven	166
The Greatness of the Lord	168
The Objective is to Finish	170
Down to the Ground	172
The Ultimate Gift	174
Pure Life	176
The Perfect Marriage	178
In Spite of Me	180
~Final Thoughts~	183
The Class of 2007	184
Pen Twin	186
The Man of God	189
About the Author	191

INTRODUCTION

The Pen God Gave Me: The Diary of My Soul is a story of redemption. This collection of poetry expresses life through the eyes of a young Black woman in today's society. This book gives an in-depth look into the problems and downfalls of modern society.

Ardreana captures vivid images of life's trials and delivers them in such a way to reach even the most mundane audience. The poetry contained in this book is very raw and confessional, allowing the reader to see the nakedness of life itself.

This is a book designed to show individuals that no matter what they may be going through, they are not alone and most of all, they can overcome.

Entry 1: The Story Behind My Life

Dear Diary,

   The story behind my life is not the easiest narrative to tell, but if my life can help the next young woman, there is nothing hindering me from telling every single word of it. Every day of my life has not been a walk in the park or a day at the beach, but it's still my story. I embrace my story because it makes me who I am. God has placed bad days in my life so that I can know how to appreciate the good days. I am strong today because of the weight that I have carried throughout this life.

Sincerely,
Ardreana

The Story Behind My Life

THE STORY BEHIND MY LIFE, it ain't no perfect breeze
If you've judged me by facial expressions...
You've been deceived

Anger behind emotions, makes laughter a hiding place
And a pencil to this paper, makes writing a driving space

It's embarrassing and shameful to do what I want to do
But, if I really didn't care, I would do what I wanted to

Meaning that I would sing
Meaning that I would dance
Meaning that I would tell my deepest love my romance

What if I'm mad or if there's anger inside?
Because I'm usually not the one to be swallowing up my pride

If ever I'm stuck between a problem and confrontation
Thoughts running through my head to remember my occupation

I'm a child of God and a Christian within
Does it make me a hypocrite when I wander into sin?

Sometimes when I'm in love and can't figure out what to do
This paper is the one whom I express my thoughts to

What if my deepest love won't think to pay attention?
Alone in a room, and all I can feel is the tension

If he doesn't pay attention, then I'll just move along
And from the way I judge a man...
Forever I'll be alone

Too many of the pretty boys are stuck on themselves
So arrogant and selfish that they only love themselves

If you look around you'll see the type of girls they flaunt
The type that gives them sex wherever and whenever they want

But the guys with the attitudes to match my perception
Bring out qualities of neglecting imperfection

Maybe I only have me and myself to blame
Since I don't look at every single situation the same

I may not do all of the things in which you think that I should
But, I have learned to discern between the bad and the good

I'M A WOMAN

I'M A WOMAN

I'm the *source* of this world

But, I often get treated as the *worst* of this world

Men pretend to love us

Placing nothing above us

Until we realize that they're messing with other lovers

Never mind that I'm a mother, a sister, a daughter,

A worker, a boss, and I'm giving plenty of orders

Men swear they're having problems

But, they don't know the definition

I face many dilemmas, but living is my ambition

And pain is repetitious

You don't know the half of things

If you think that love means

Money and diamond rings

Then you're sadly mistaken

And I'm here to inform you

That money can't pay for all the crap that I've been through

I'M A WOMAN

I bleed twelve months of the year

So evidently, a man is the least of my fear

I'M A WOMAN

I carry a child for nine months

So why should I fall for a grill of gold fronts

I'M A WOMAN

I sweep, mop, and dust a dirty home

While he's out chasing girls, when he has **a woman** at home

I'M A WOMAN

I demand *every ounce* of my respect

Although I end up doing jobs that little boys neglect

I'M A WOMAN

So why amount to boys expectations

A thin model chic with pretty eye pigmentation

And for your information...

I know that I was blessed,

With thick hips, thick lips, and a full set of breast

I'M A WOMAN

So, **every woman** is in me

A woman is strong enough to set a caged bird free

I'm not saying that a man means nothing to me,

Because I love a strong brother with strong personality

But **a woman...**

A woman is a *gift* to this Earth

It's a blessing being **a woman**

And that's far from a curse

I'M A WOMAN

I won't stop until my battle is over

But not only am I a woman...

I'M A FULL GROWN SOLDIER

STEREOTYPE OF A BLACK WOMAN

I know what they say about me,

She's **A BLACK WOMAN**,

She'll never be free

From the articles, they wrote saying Blacks don't read

To the rumors, they spread saying...

I'll never succeed

I know they probably say, I'm always waiting on a man

But God, is the **only man** with my life in His hands

And I know they probably say, I'm always in court

Having babies by different men...

For some child support

White girls up front, Black girls behind

And they criticize the ones in the welfare line

It's a shame that some of these brothers notice my behind

Before they notice anything,

That I instill in my mind

Am I a waste of time, because **I'M A BLACK WOMAN**?
You'd better clear the path whenever you see me coming

I'm a legacy...
The seed of a Beautiful Black Rose
I acknowledge that fact, from my head to my toes

Black skin, African roots, I love this African culture
I love my African Sisters and my African Brothers
I love my African Fathers and my African Mothers
So do you think the worst of me, because I'm this color?

So don't STEREOTYPE me, if you truly don't know
Because my Black Sisters and I,
Are steady running the show

We made it this far,
Therefore, we must be good for something
But I'm not your...
STEREOTYPE OF ANY BLACK WOMAN

STRENGTH

STRENGTH comes from a personality,
That has maneuvered through life with rationality
It makes no difference of their nationality
Strong people call shots, without technicalities

We all have abnormalities...
But, we must use them to an advantage
So when we're thrown curve balls in life...
We can manage

I handle my problems, and not let my problems handle me
I've learned to deal with love, life, death, as well as family
So what another human thinks about me is like a fan to me
Blown into the wind and cut off like electricity

While I'm here, I'll strive to make a legacy for myself
I'll never leave a job to burden anyone else

I'm mighty, I'm strong, and God has my back
I've fought a million battles...
A million times, I've been attacked

I know for a fact, that I'm a **strong** Black woman,
Because my feet are blackened and blistered…
From this race that I've been running

STRENGTH lies in these eyes, so as I envision my size
I'll never stoop to have to use the *strength* between these thighs

STRENGTH lies in my lips, so I speak boldly when you trip
But I'll never slip to have to use the *strength* within these hips

STRENGTH lies in my nose, so take a whiff of this rose
Don't envy the fact, that God has blessed me to grow

STRENGTH lies in these ears, though I have heard of no fears
I will still outstretch my hands to sanitize in your tears

STRENGTH lies in my neck, so before I make a bet,
I'll be sure that I gamble from my own paycheck

STRENGTH lies in these breast, so whenever you test
I'll be sure to remove every drop of stress from my chest

STRENGTH lies in my stomach, so if ever I should vomit
I'm woman enough to clean the mess up like Comet

STRENGTH lies in every single one of my cuts,

Determined to let men know that...

WE ARE WOMEN AND NOT SLUTS!

STRENGTH lies in the curves of these hips and these thighs,

So while using this section of my body...I'm wise

The use is for my lover, husband, and friend

I'm an excellent young woman

Not a one-night stand

STRENGTH lies in these calves, ankles, and heels

This arch, these toes, this switch...

IT KILLS!

Stop for a second...

Am I stronger than you imagined?

I'm already in the game,

WHILE THE OTHERS ARE STILL AT PRACTICE!

MY IDENTITY

Poetic blood in my veins

So, I sunk in my fangs

Just to get a taste of the emotions...

That helped me to define my name

"Who am I?" Is what I asked

Amnesia had kicked in

No anesthetics

Pain times ten

Being born was my sin

But, hold your tongue dear child

No freedom of expression...

Bottle it up

Store it at heart

Don't make any confessions

Let it drift you into a sea of major depression

But I couldn't...

I rebelled

I burst the bottles across the pavement

And asked my own set of questions

Why should I shut my mouth and remain in depression?

Couldn't the story behind my life...

Become someone else's blessing?

I'm still alive, when they're others who have died

So why shouldn't I let you stick a finger into the pond of tears,

I've cried?

So I step on a few toes to flatten the path for young women

Young and timid

I earned **MY IDENTITY**

Because it surely wasn't given

I've made mistakes

I've been broken into tiny pieces,

Like glass plates

And now, I know what it takes to make the move and state,

"CHECK MATE"

Being strong was my fate

I thank God that I'm still here
Without a fear, I stand firm
Yes, I stand firm without a tear

I trust my Creator
I adore His every plan...

MY IDENTITY
I'm His child
Therefore, I owe fear to no man

THE WORDS I WRITE

Beneath this skin...

Behind these eyes...

Lies something much more than a tired mind

Body worn down,

Blood seeking through my pores...

From my forehead, more than sweat pours

I trust in God, and that's more than enough for me

To climb over hurdles and plow through weeds

That's enough for me to overcome all of my hard times

Enough for me to end up in the Hall of Fame for written lines

So, **I WRITE** more than lines

I WRITE more than stanzas

I WRITE more than lyrics and verses that develops like cancer

I WRITE more than songs

I WRITE more than poetry

I WRITE more than rivers of tears that flow up under me

I WRITE more than stories
I WRITE more than essays
I WRITE more than life that lives within an empty page

I WRITE more than love
I WRITE more than hate
Because **MY WRITINGS** are a fetus unborn,
Yet taking shape

MY WRITINGS are the death of fear
A new beginning
MY WRITINGS are a born again Christian,
Restrained from sinning

I WRITE my heart
Drenched in blood and beating strong
I WRITE SO THAT MY WORDS CAN LIVE ON

FOLLOW YOUR DREAMS

Last night, I dozed off for a brief moment...

And at that moment,

I noticed that there was a road beneath my feet

Ahead was all that I could see

Along with an area filled with unoccupied space

Excluding the space of me

So, I slowly followed the path

Didn't know if I could last

Or if the end would be my hope for a hopeful aftermath

To the left of me came someone...

Who I thought would be the death of me

Holding on to my arm and looking in my eyes helplessly

She said, "I need you to be here for me;

Never give me your absence,

Let your presence linger here,

Forever...Everlasting

I'm your siblings, your father, your friends, your mother."

Underneath it all...
To the left lied my struggle

I looked to the right
As the peak had reached midnight
I lost sight...Colorblind
My world was black and white

Scenes played like a television in my mind
But there were only unrecognizable moments
Maybe before my time

The girl I saw, favored me
Uncircumcised beauty

In other words, nothing touched
Her natural hung loosely

I was saddened by her tears
A look so upsetting
She saw me and she asked,
"Ma'am is there something that you're regretting?"

Initially, I lied
Then I began to cry
The dream took a transition
A nurse screamed, "Doctor, will this girl die?"

He said, "I don't know? It's not my decision;
the woman who brought her in has to stitch up
her final incision."

It was I, who had brought her there
None of it was fair
I realized that she was the one who had gotten me there

To the right was that little girl screaming for help
To save her from death
However, I had to remember myself

"Don't look back!"
Is what the voice yelled inside of my head

"Do you want to see that place in life at where you
could've been dead?

The past is the past

Leave it behind

LET IT GO!

Return no more

Walk until your heels become sore

I am what lie ahead of you

Listen closely to me

I will help you to be happy,

Being what you desire to be

I'm your future

Solo or with a team

Unseen, I'm not always what I seem

But what I say, is what I mean,

FOLLOW Me and I'll reveal myself as **YOUR DREAM**."

GIVING ALL BUT ME

I'm all out of **GIVING**
There's **nothing** left to give
They say eventually you'll reap within...
The type of life you live

I've reaped many things,
Tragedy times seven
They say just wait until Judgment Day
Well, what if somehow I miss Heaven?

I know it doesn't sound pleasant
But, I'm just being honest
Am I speaking as the eldest?
Or do I sound like the youngest?

Does my choice of words hold strength?
Or am I a vessel of weak?
Whichever way you perceive it...Its fine,
Because I'll still end up with...ME

DAYDREAM

I want to live the life that I **DAYDREAM** about
I want to be the epitome of where you used to place your doubt

I want to see the places of where I've only dreamed of going
I want to be the star, of a sold out showing

I want the world to fall in love with every single word I write
I want to recite my poetry...
Beneath the lint of bright spotlights

I want to tell those who never believed that I could make it,
Something so derogative that they'd have no choice...
But to hate this

I want to abolish **all negativity** from the mind,
Of all young women who will never be able to find
The **positivity** that they so rightfully deserve
From their mothers and fathers who refuse to put them first

I want to shoot this hatred and bury it in the dirt
I want to tell Jesus that SIN has corrupted His church

I want to let Him know that most abortions are given,
Because it takes a decade for a pregnant teen to be FORGIVEN

I want to tell Him that most young men die,
Because they're **too ashamed** to let the world know that...
They cry

On Judgment Day, when Jesus takes a look at my life,
I hope it's more than A GAMBLE OF HYPOCRISY'S DICE

I hope He's not the man people have made Him out to be
I hope He judges me for what He knows...
And not for what the world has chosen to see

I hope that He takes the time to look me in the eyes,
And understand the reason...
That I hid behind lies

I hope He judges you, the same way you judged me
I hope He sees your face and eliminates His Grace and Mercy

I hope He sees you aspiring to do His job
I hope He returns the joy to me, that you have chosen to rob

So today is the day that I house clean
And rid myself of those who tried to **kill my dream**

Because I want to live the life that I **DAYDREAMED** about
And no longer be the epitome...
Of where you choose to place your doubt

INNER SELF

I want the world to see me

Do you really believe me?

I hate attention

It always takes away from the real me

When I'm lonely

At least I know who I am

Alone is where I discovered the fact that...

I'm my own biggest fan

The real me was there the first time,

I held a microphone in my hand

The real me felt my nervousness,

The real me supported my plan

She was there the first time I spoke on Poetry Night

Trembles in my voice, afraid I wouldn't sound right

She was there in the 4th Grade,

As I stood before The School Body

And delivered the poem entitled,

The Faith Inside of a Slave's Bible

She was there when I was a little girl...
Cutting pictures from magazines
Writing my own interpretation...
Of what I thought that it should mean

She's here with me now,
As the world drowns in doubt
She believes in me...
She knows what I'm about

She'll be there at the end of the day,
Consoling me as I rejuvenate...
From the hate

I don't ever have to worry about her going anywhere,
She'll never leave me lonely...
She's my **INNER SELF**

BLOOD TYPE: POETRY

Pen and paper is my transfusion

My notebook is my blood bank

I have very few donors

Because **poetry** is a rare **blood type**

If ever I am dying from a circumstance that involves...

The giving of blood

Tell the doctor to open my notebook

And let the blood stained pages...

From the inner soul of that notebook,

Drain into my body

And only then, shall I live

Entry 11: The Media

Dear Diary,

    As I look around, I find that many of my peers are being taken by the media. The media consist of sex, drugs, and violence. Every day, young minds are drawn into what they see on television. The real reason a child behaves the way that he/she does is because children often imitate what they see. Raising a child is all about putting positive examples and role models before their eyes. It saddens me to know that so many Americans are letting the media raise their children.

                      Sincerely,
                      Ardreana

THE MEDIA

Has it ever dawned on you that the things which I pursue,
Are the things that I want, and not the things I ask of you?

Hypothetically speaking, am I not your expectations?
Well, neither am I your servant, or any other relation

THE MEDIA wants us to believe that they're perfect
So, we buy into the lies that they sugar coat on the surface

The girls want to look like the models in the videos
And the boys want to sound like the rappers in the stereos

Many of us are guilty of boosting degrading radio
When the message I'm spitting
You really don't seem to hear me though

It's not that I'm hating, but if you take this information
And look behind the scenes,
Then you'll see the hallucination

Many of my Sisters show a loyal dedication
To putting themselves in difficult and awkward situations

Then they wonder why,
The brothers are calling them different names
When they're offering their bodies,
As paying the price of fame

If you're taking it as a game...
Then you should seriously check yourself,
Because neglecting morality is disrespecting yourself

And many of my Brothers are no better than the Sisters
But they deem themselves worthy...
Of wearing the title Mister

They wonder why these Sisters are scandalizing their game,
Calling us sluts and whores
But, can barely spell their own name

You can take it as the same because this analysis is untamed
But, it's not intended to bring a life of shame

I'm only telling it like it is,
But you can take it how you want to
Since you're grown, I have no right to tell you what to do

But, sometimes we often think that television is an actuality
That is when we need to snap ourselves back into reality

There is nothing authentic about the glamour of TV
So instead of being like them,
I would rather be like me

EVEN A MONSTER CRIES

Yesterday I told myself, that I'd never write again
Because I wrote a million words...
To which a million people took offense

I feel like a **MONSTER** on the inside

It must be more than just a feeling,
I guess that's the reason,
No one really wants me living

My Black friends think I'm a sell-out...
For listening to more than R&B and Rap
Said I must've gotten lost on life's road map

Said I must've forgotten where I come from
So I become numb to myself...For them
And hold back these words of mine
So that I won't feel like a **MONSTER**
It seems as though I'm a **MONSTER**
I feel like a **MONSTER** on the inside

It must be more than just a feeling,
I guess that's the reason that,
No one really wants me living

My White friends think I'm a racist...
When I talk about the struggles of being Black
They start believing that I'm...
Issuing an attack

They think I'm packed to the rim with anger
Two steps away from danger
They get offended when I say,
"Because I'm Black, I'm dangerous to a stranger."

They say to me, "You shouldn't talk about it."
Because they believe it's only a part of the past...
And that I should just forget about it

So I become numb to myself...For them
And hold back these words of mine
So that I won't feel like a **MONSTER**
It seems as though I'm a **MONSTER**
I feel like a **MONSTER** on the inside

It must be more than just a feeling,
I guess that's the reason,
No one really wants me living

My religious friends think I'm going to Hell...
When I don't agree with them

Said if I didn't believe every word of what they believe...
Then I must not be one of them

And now they believe that in their crowd I don't fit
Said that they're right and I'm wrong,
So I must be a hypocrite

So I become numb to myself...For them
And hold back these words of mine
So that I won't feel like a **MONSTER**
It seems as though I'm a **MONSTER**
I feel like a **MONSTER** on the inside

It must be more than just a feeling,
I guess that's the reason,
No one really wants me living

My unreligious friends think I'm judging them...
When I don't participate in the things that they do
They think I don't have a clue,
About what they're going through

They say I should participate
Or gather my belongings and shy away
I feel like they take offense to every single word I say

So I become numb to myself...For them
And hold back these words of mine
So that I won't feel like a **MONSTER**
It seems as though I'm a **MONSTER**
I feel like a **MONSTER** on the inside

It must be more than just a feeling,
*I guess I must be a **MONSTER**...*
For not judging others for being different

When I see people,
I don't see WHAT they are
I only see WHO they are

I don't ask them their business before they tell me
I guess I'm a **MONSTER...**
For finding every single life to be compelling
I feel like a **MONSTER** on the inside

It must be more than just a feeling,
I guess that's the reason,
No one really wants me living

So I stopped writing
And at the moment, that I decided not to write...
My inner being died
I'M A **MONSTER**
But even I didn't know that...
MONSTERS HELD TEARY EYES

WHEN

WHEN will we as women educate ourselves?
Not on Philosophy, Geography, or Biology
But on *Self-Respect*

We have become so entangled in this web of cosmetology
Becoming vain as if we're trapped in a game of Monopoly
Letting men obtain our squares, as if they own our property
Giving birth to innocent souls and raising them improperly

Allowing the male species to ignore our brains,
And focus on our bodies
Ultimately altering the sexual experience into…
Some type of hobby

Stepping into us boldly like a hotel lobby
And **WHEN** they're done,
They invite their friends to pour into the party

I often sit and wonder why so many pregnancies
Are pushed into young women body's unexpectedly
How can I expect a man to possess respect for me?
WHEN I spread these legs for him non-hesitantly

I often wonder why we give men the option,
To insert themselves inside of us and take our soul...
Like an adoption

Draining their misery until they form a concoction,
Neglected to be protected being filled with their toxins

Recklessly, why can't I take the time to care for me?
Why have I resorted to letting men drive me recklessly?

WHEN will the moment come?
WHEN will I allow them to cease?
I guess it's **WHEN...**
I've tested **POSITIVE FOR HIV**

DEVILS

DEVILS in disguise

So many **DEVILS** in my eyes

Dismiss yourself **DEVIL**

I don't want to hear your lies

Because of **DEVILS**

A million women cry

And solely because of **DEVILS**

A million women die

Spiritually they're dead,

Because **DEVILS** fill their heads

With stereotypes and notions that they have to spread their legs

As for the babies of this nation

DEVILS often over take em'

They are immaturely grown

Therefore it doesn't take much to break em'

The media rapes em' and morality escapes em'

So instead of picking em' up

We intellects degrade em'

Intellectually spoken, I'm intellectually hoping
That instead of stunting growth...
Poets would focus more on growing

Growing the nation's children and healing these broken spirits
Teaching this whole nation not to sell their soul for a living

Rappers are poets with such unique expressions
But, let's face it,
Rap seems to be making no progression

Instead of progressing power through the mic
They're too busy telling us that our wrongs...are our rights

And our rights are our wrongs
DEVILS enter the mind by the words of these songs

My words are a bomb, that haven't been detonated yet
And since I haven't gone to jail...
They haven't imitated me yet

If this was a song, I know they wouldn't play this
And because of what you accept, I really shouldn't say this

My heart made this bed and encouraged me to lay this

I say what I feel, with no desire to be famous

Jesus loves me unconditionally

So please explain what popularity should mean to me?

I will never sell my soul for the price of fame

Because only the **DEVIL** wins...

When you're playing his game

CONFESSIONS OF DIRTY MONEY

(A True Story of Prostitution Part I)

I'm a prostitute, but not by choice
Deaf and Dumb for way too long;
No ear, No voice

Maybe I'm not a prostitute, maybe I'm just a whore
I don't charge for my services
I wait til they beg for more

Maybe I am a prostitute because that's just how I get em'
Let em' feast on me for free, until I make em' my victim

That's how I gain my power, yet lose my soul
They all flock to see me,
Strip my innocence on a pole

When I hypnotize the faithful, they began to criticize
Because they know that, I can jeopardize...
The judgment of their lives

I break up homes, husbands and wives
Parents keep me away from their children as they do knives

But they can't because I'm everywhere
Every corner without a care
I'm determined to overtake the brain...
Which lies beneath every hair

Good girls, bad girls, first girls, last girls
Healed girls, hurt girls, street girls, church girls

Doesn't matter who they are, I make them all follow me
Because I tell em' every day that every man wants a freak

There's no such thing as holding on if you're not putting out
Men love what I can swallow, not what comes out of my mouth

They only listen to me when I tell them their fantasy
If I tell them the truth, then I'd be giving it up for free

Every little boy, I let them know what they've been missing
I get em' when they're young
Because that's the only time they listen

I tell them to cheat on their girlfriends
Pass the cocaine to my hand
What has love done for you?
Live your life on one-night stands

I belong to you, so smoke the other brother on the spot
I only mess with ballers, so lie about everything you got
Say you drink Patrone by the shot and brag about the riches;
That'll make you hot

And don't forget about the tricks
We actually answer to it now
Gives us some type of superiority
But I still don't know how

I'm where you get your pleasure
When you're frustrated with the world
On my back or on my knees, I'm still your favorite girl

When you grow into a man
I know you'll see me a little different
Use to brag about me to your boys
Now you're sneaking me through the kitchen

But don't you dare speak of me as anything short of a lady
You're the blame for this
Because I'm what your generation made me

Don't even waste your time and energy trying to save me
Adults do what they want
You should have raised me from a baby

I give it to you boldly and I honestly don't care
But, I still say it's not fair to label me a nightmare

I'm the lyric on your paper; I'm the freestyle in your head
I'm the reason that my elders say,
The industry is dead

I'm that 20 dollar bill that you spent to see my show
I'm a stripper of words, and the mic is my pole

To all virgin poets, think before you lose
Because I'd hate to see your name under the prostitutes of muse

CONFESSIONS OF DIRTY MONEY

(A True Story of Prostitution Part II)

I've returned to tell part-two of life as a prostitute

Why lie about my life, when I'm striving to tell the truth

I could care less if a child ruins their youth

How does that concern me, when the parent is you?

My records are in your cars, on your shelves,

And in your stereos

I want you to follow me, but I'll never be your hero

When you've reached the state that you're bound to come back,

I'll play on your emotions until your conscience attack

I never give a second thought to how I entered your house,

Because you never think before inserting things in my mouth

Even though you front as though I'm the downfall of this world

You still haven't denied that I'm your favorite girl

Every young woman should be just like me

No respect for how I live

Classified as a freak

I create lesbians...

Good men don't exist

I'm responsible for the acceptance of being labeled a trick

No remorse for my actions...Not even a little bit

I've dealt with men from the pen...

To men in the pulpit

So if you dare to challenge me, I must dare to let you see

That I can cause the blind to envision

What they'd never expect to see

I bring havoc upon lives

Make husbands beat wives

Put bullets in cerebellums

Perform surgeries with knives

I'm only claiming to be the things your generation made me

There will never be a way to play with my body safely

If I attempt to live right, I think you'd find it quite funny

Even a dummy is aware,

That I'm only after your money

I was poor and homeless, so I sold you my soul
Because I knew you'd pay to see me...
Strip my innocence on a pole

So I stand before a mic every night of the week
I dishonor my talent by the lyrics I speak

I'm the pen to the paper, the flow to the mic
The sex, drugs, and violence introduced to your life

I'm the music on your radio, the disc inside your stereo
The bars and adlibs that you spit inside the studio

Attention all poets, think before you choose
Or be placed under the dishonorable prostitutes of muse

HOW A CRACK HEAD IS MADE

It starts as a seed, and grows within time
Then broken to a point, where it can further be refined

Powder, white girl, cocaine is nothing good
Regardless of what it's called
It's in every Black neighborhood

One young man's story stuck to me like glue
Don't judge or shake your head, because it could happen to you

Do judge for yourself whether this is pure fiction
Imagine **CRACK COCAINE** cooked
In your grandmother's kitchen

Granny never would've guessed…
That those things were in her house
But what is a man to do being born with…
No *silver spoon* in his mouth

He was always told, "You can't!"
And never told, "You can!"
He then tuned the world out and declared himself a man

Cocaine, a teaspoon, a measuring cup, a pan, and baking soda
Determined to make a few bucks
Just hoping that this start,
Would bring him up on his luck

So he poured about **an ounce of cocaine** in a cup
He carefully added the right amount of baking soda
He boiled, he cooled, and his poverty was over

He drained it, he cut it, and he had produced his rocks
Chef Drug-ardee was done, so he punched out on the clock

He often used color as an excuse for not living right
I guess he blamed this **CRACK**,
Therefore, he cooked it til it was white

For guys in my neighborhood, I guess life was much harder
Dummies in the classroom...
But in the lab they were much smarter

May not have meant anything to you
But in the hood, he was a star
Distributing like a soldier in the Columbian Drug War

Drugs are not success; drugs won't get you far
However, you would still destroy a life,
To put rims on your car

I'd like to tell the story that you'd never dare to tell
How to make a million dollars by sending your soul to Hell

Financially he was successful, but spiritually he failed
He was heartbroken by a woman,
Who was a part of his clientele

I'd like to tell the story of an intelligent young woman
Transformed into a junkie, but she never saw it coming

She was a college graduate who was very fond of her books
Beautiful little lady, very easy on her looks

Didn't care about drugs and never desired beer bottles
Thick in all of the right places, could have been a super model

Met a man and had some kids; four to be exact
Fell in love with that man,
Until he started dealing with **CRACK**

He pimped tons of women...I'm only stating the facts
So cold hearted...that he paid each of them in **CRACK**

Insecure about himself, so he laid hands on his wife
The decision to marry this man...
Destroyed this young woman's life

He told her that he was sorry
He told her that he loved her
Nevertheless, that didn't stop him from feeding **cocaine**...
To his children's mother

The kids were neglected
The situation had turned bad
More lines were in the house
Than a pajama set in plaid

Blood is thicker than water...
So this young woman's brother
Made a vow to himself,
To smoke a hole through her lover

Some mourned his death and others thanked the Lord
Black male, 5'11...Lying down at the morgue

Kids went to grandmother and mother went to rehab
Granny did her best raising kids with no dad

Rehab had been completed; mother was now clean
She gained custody of her oldest son,
When he turned sixteen

When this young man went to school,
His mother cleaned the house
The moment she cleaned his room
She sniffed it out like a mouse

She thought that she was strong and that she could resist
But lost all control, as that rock was clenched in her fist

As he returned from school and headed upstairs in a dash
Opened the door, pulled his Glock,
And caught someone in his stash

Tears streamed down his face as he noticed it was his mom
Then and there he knew that the worst was yet to come
This child's next decision was the most difficult thing to see
This explains why a **dope boy** isn't the easiest thing to be

He said within himself, "If anything must be,
instead of my mother on the block,
I'd rather her get it from me."

This type of situation goes on every day
This is one of the ways that...
A CRACK HEAD IS MADE

HOW DO YOU STOP A HEART FROM BLEEDING?

They see my lips moving, but they hear nothing
They can't see that they're losing
Or should I say winning nothing

They're focused on the hell, and not the blessing
And here I am playing mother,
A constant routine of stressing

I pray that things get better in the deeper pits of the mind
It's like a tumor's pushing on the cornea,
Leaving the eyes blind

Why not see that the war is against self
Defeated personality
Finish line that equals death

Buzzed off of anger, high compared to meth
Scratchy picture resembles,
A throat containing strep

It's upsetting
I make an effort to show them that they're children
But the blindness makes them want to handle
Grown men's business

Sometimes I wonder, if they'll live long enough to understand
Or if they'll end up taking residency...
In a casket with praying hands

It's disturbing fighting a war for no apparent reason
You can put a bandage on a scar,
BUT...
HOW DO YOU STOP A HEART FROM BLEEDING?

NEKA'S SONG

Born to the streets, she was born to the streets
Forced to fight this war against the harm in the streets

Her blood is as sweet as bitter wine
Her bed is as clean as that of the swine

At no fault of her own does she behave as she does
Her fate is overwhelming,
She doesn't know how to love

Cursed at birth,
Born with hands that fit evil gloves
She looks down knowing that her limit is not above

NEKA'S SONG is as beautiful as ugly
NEKA'S SONG...the lyrics sing, "Nobody loves me."
NEKA'S SONG has a beat that never trusts me
NEKA'S SONG is as beautiful as ugly

Raised by only Gran,
She was passed along as a child,
And now she stands as second-hand

Gran soon dies and then she's forced into the streets
Destined for doom...
When you're born with traces of cocaine on your feet

As it lies inside of her gum,
She's attracted to the streets
And the day will soon come
That you'll see the crumbs on her teeth

Born a crack baby; cocaine in the blood
To achieve the highest goals,
She'll have to climb through the mud

She's hindered...
Being hurt by her own family members
Life as cold as midnight in December

Impregnated by an uncle and forced into abortion
Life is a bit too much...
When you're given this size of a portion

Later, she has a baby...
But, who is the baby's father?

Similar to her mother
Neka doesn't know her father
Neka's just a lamb being led to the slaughter

But, **her song** is deeper than the rivers
And as beautiful as the daughters

The wind that blows golden leaves, in Fall weather
Sings **NEKA'S SONG**
And binds the notes together

NEKA'S SONG is strong, because to be less than thirteen
And able to endure the brightness of pain's beam
She stands out in the rain
And lifts her voice strongly, until she reaches her fame

NEKA'S SONG will be beautiful the day she overcomes
Then she can let the world know,
That her VICTORY has been won

NEKA'S SONG is as ugly as beauty
Because **NEKA'S SONG** travels deep enough...
TO MOVE ME

BABY

She was easy like Sunday morning,

Freaky and often horny

Far from a role model, or anything you'd find adoring

She was whoring in the streets,

With the desire to get busy with every man she meets

THE NEIGHBORHOOD FREAK

Was never taught that love is in the mind, and not the penis

Was never taught that commitment is in the heart,

And not the semen

There she lay screaming on a delivery table

Disconnected from the world like some unpaid cable

The lines on the EKG seems kind of unstable

And now the least of her worries is being tied to a label

Nine months had passed,

No medical care

What could've been avoided,

Is now her worst night mare

The doctor states words that she could never forgive,
"One of you has to die and the other one has to live."

Preparing for transition into eternal sleep
She feels she owes it to her daughter to be more than just a freak
Testing is done in an effort to seek
More from between her legs than just a vaginal leak

Mother is now dead
BABY is now screaming
BABY looks healthy
But, the **BABY** soul is bleeding

Mommy soul was bleeding,
But Mommy was never tested
So was **BABY** given a curse?
Or was **BABY** given a blessing?

Mommy sincerely thought that **BABY** would be safe
But, how could it be so...
When **BABY** was born with AIDS?

BEING BLACK

I would like to inform you of the things that you do
They reflect back to the things that your ancestors went through

And yet you sit around, thinking it's all good
Desiring to be bad, because you grew up in the hood

Well bad is what got a lot of my brothers in the grave
And bad never protected that life,
That could've been saved

Bad is the reason that your mother is crying
And bad is the reason,
You're in the hospital dying

Well if you think I'm lying, then find another source
Because I tell it like it is...
And I do it with no remorse

You have no other choice, if you want to live peacefully
And truth is...
The only thing that I fight to release from me

Take a stand without violence,

Like Dr. Martin Luther King...

Without wasting time fighting about irrelevant things

The colors that were fought for, were due to discrimination

The colors being fought for now are for hood representation

In the streets getting beaten with tear gas and water hoses

And back in those days, being free was their only focus

Now we're turning up our noses with no intent to vote

Well, take my advice and follow a different note

BEING BLACK is a song that I proudly sing

Because **BEING BLACK** is a blessing,

From my Heavenly King

NEW FOUND RESPECT

To all of my Black brothers who reside in this country

For years you've been ridiculed

And viewed as gorillas and monkeys

But now, you can look anyone square in the eye

And say,

"I'll be proud to be a Black man until the day I die."

Let them know that you know more than...

How to put weed in a sack

Tell the critics that you would rather have...

Education than crack

Let them know that you are more than America's stats

You are not simply a man

Look in the mirror...

You're Black!

When your own try to oppress you...

By locking you down in the game

Put the bullets away,

And defend your territory with your brain

When a Sister tell you that...
You're only good for child support
Tell that Sister that one day...
You'll be the Judge of that court

When your Preacher tells you that...
You'll only amount to a thug
Tell the Preacher you're destined to be a doctor...
Who heals patients with love

When your teacher tells you that...
You'll be in jail pretty soon
Tell the teacher one day,
You'll be an astronaut on the moon

They often say that...
You'll only become rich if you rap
Don't let it sink into your mind,
And leave your abilities handicapped

When a Sister like me tells you that...
You are who she represents
Proudly accept being a Black man...
Because you can be a President

HISTORY

A Black man is in the White House Mansion
Obama won for President, but will he end up like John Hanson

The name doesn't sound familiar,
Because no one really taught it
But, if you would've researched **HISTORY**
Then maybe you could've caught it

First President, *a dollar bill* with a face
George Washington was the rumor
But, John Hanson was the case

HISTORY books continue to teach lies and deception
Developing ignorance to form a slavery conception

If 40 acres and a mule forced you to believe that you're free
Then go ahead and dig a grave,
Because that's where you're destined to be

From the grass in my yard to the dirt on Capitol Hill
Ask the government why we rarely see a 2-dollar bill

If you turn the bill over and view the men around the table

The African American among the Caucasians...

Would leave **HISTORY** unstable

Many of the minorities are material for college

But, the government would rather invest in incarceration,

Than knowledge

You can be African American, White, Asian, or Korean

Mexican, Dominican, Native American, or Philippian

God is not concerned about the color of our skins,

So why are we so set upon doing each other in?

HISTORY is deep

HISTORY is real

If you don't know your **HISTORY**

Then your life has been sealed

If I'm condemned by my **HISTORY**

I'm exalted by the light

Because Heaven has nothing to do with my being...

BLACK or WHITE

WHERE HAVE ALL THE BLACK MEN GONE?

WHERE HAVE ALL THE BLACK MEN GONE?

What are they doing?

Why are they so ignorant to the fact that we need them?

WHERE HAVE THEY GONE?

Caged like animals, locked behind bars

Given to the streets, loss to gang wars

Occupying graveyards, occupying jail yards

Vainly living the life of a ghetto superstar

WHERE HAVE ALL OF THE BLACK MEN GONE?

What are they doing?

Why are they so ignorant to the fact that we need them?

WHERE HAVE THEY GONE?

On television defining a woman as something to degrade

Unaware of the fact that we're the ones who were raped

Slaves to our masters, forced to run faster

Having babies by men,

Who would never raise a bastard

Dreams destroyed in an unforgiving nation
Born with skin that automatically declines a job application

Held back because we lack the opportunity
To fight our way through bullets, as we search for unity

That we could only find as we dress in black
And step into a church
Filled with teary eyes and wet faces
Speaking words that have yet to stop the continuation...
Of Black men falling beyond the dirt

So when someone asks the question,
WHERE HAVE ALL THE BLACK MEN GONE?

I'll ask the questions,
When will all the prisons close?
And when will morticians have to find a full-time job
And bury people as a part-time job?

So until then, we will never end
This desperate search for all of...
AMERICA'S BLACK MEN

ENSLAVED MINDS

Golden sunshine on the skin of a Black child
Is like calcium to the bones
Blackened soles from walking a thousand miles
This journey of mine, I've walked alone

I guess that sun did me no good
If it did, I wouldn't still be misunderstood

When I don't eat from the same table...
As corn bread colored children
I get to feeling like this ol' life ain't really worth a living

Shivering under the midnight sky
Gotta find some shelter fo' I die

Gunshots roaring thru the woods
Covered in blood, I'd be no good

Though they were slaves a long time ago,
We *still* got a long way to go

Yes, they were slaves way back in time
But, we're still **ENSLAVED, JUST IN OUR MINDS**

A CHILD WORTH CRYING FOR

A CHILD WORTH A TEAR is a child born into the world

Fear, hate, terror, and pain

Are all forced upon our boys and girls

I've seen children cry,

But not for candy and chips

From blackened eyes, bruised behinds, broken bones,

And busted lips

Do we stand by and say nothing?

Or do we step up and speak for need?

We pray for ourselves at leisure

But, how many times for our children do we plead?

If we don't help our children,

We'll never see a future

Wounds are opened from emotional damage

But, who shall provide the suture

Sometimes I cry at night for a child...

WHO CAN'T CRY FOR HIS OR HERSELF

Some never make it to grievance,

Because some first make it to death

And as God be a witness to my heart
He knows that my prayer is sincere...

For every child that fears
For every child that hurts
I'M HERE TO SHED A TEAR!

TAKE THE TIME

TAKE THE TIME to notice,
The personality behind the child
The cry, the laugh, the good, the bad,
The joy behind the smile

TAKE THE TIME to see,
The talent in the hands
The future of a woman
The destiny of a man

TAKE THE TIME to hear,
Just what they have to say
Don't let the exigencies of life,
Cause their gifts to fade away

TAKE THE TIME to enjoy them,
For they are very precious

TAKE THE TIME to set them down,
And teach them life's many lessons

Blessings are what they are,
So don't let them waste away
Pray for them, mentor them,
And watch them day by day

TAKE THE TIME to give to them,
The life that they deserve
Place them in your heart
Because they truly are the world

DEAD MESSENGER

Hard to digest this feeling, I'm feeling

Stuck giving all of my heart as my death,

Makes a killing off of my living

I pour my words out to a dead crowd

I'm a writer now,

This would have made my mother proud

But, I guess that all of that was in my head,

Because they won't appreciate the message

Until the **MESSENGER IS DEAD**

So, I shake my head

Entry III: Beauty

Dear Diary,

   Society can really get a girl down sometimes, but I have learned that long hair, pretty eyes, and size six jeans is not the definition of true beauty. I have learned that the spirit is what makes a person beautiful. No matter what society says, I know that spiritual beauty will always outshine physical beauty.

                             Sincerely,
                             Ardreana

BEAUTY

BEAUTY can't really be defined
It is something that we can't see with the naked eye
But that doesn't change the fact,
That we can't help but to be aware of its presence

It is the underlying difference between,
COSMETOLOGY and SPIRITUALITY
PHYSICALITY versus PERSONALITY
AND a HOUSE versus A HOME

In comparison to skin and bones,
It is like nails and wood
It protects what's inside

Inside of a being
Is a soul that FEELS and HURTS
REJOICES and PRAISES
LEARNS and TEACHES

The body can only do what the soul allows
Therefore, **BEAUTY** is a reflection of what's inside
But, **BEAUTY** can't solely be defined as a reflection

When I smile, **I'm beautiful**
When I laugh, **I'm beautiful**
When I cry **am I no longer beautiful**?
GOD FORBID!

I remain beautiful through it all
I'm beautiful even when angered beyond measures

I'm beautiful
Not because of the mascara on my lashes,
Or the lipstick on my lips
But, for the simple fact that I'm who I am

And I love who I am...
Many may hate me
Within themselves, they have found their own reason
Regardless of, at the end of the day
I remain beautiful

Those who hate me are upset,
Because they lack **BEAUTY**
They smile, but because it's not genuine
They lack **BEAUTY**
They may laugh, but behind their laughter is jealousy

Because they are not laughing as of one who has found joy
But as of one who rejoices at someone else's expense
They continue to lack **BEAUTY**

When they cry, I don't sympathize;
Not because I don't care,
But because when I see the tears in their eyes
I am confident that they are reaping the prize

That they have so diligently striven for
When they are angry, I can't understand them

Not because I hate them
But, because they had no remorse as they caused pain for others
Because they are human...I forgive them

I'm intelligent enough to know that people make mistakes
Sometimes they make mistakes that take much more than...
A toolbox to fix

I admit, that I'm broken
The repairs require more than just a few earned dollars
An iron around the collar
Or soap and hot water to sanitize in the shower

It's hard, but I love them
And that is what makes **me beautiful**

Out of all the things in this world that are found to be useful
The Lord has used me to define what it means…
To be beautiful

BLESSED BE THE MAN WHO FINDS A WOMAN LIKE ME

Blessed be the man who finds a woman like me
Wise, not in mine own eyes,
But God helps me to see

If I seek the Kingdom first,
Then all other things will be added
I'm not searching for a man,
You can write that in your tablet

The plan is to trust God to send who He wants in my life
I'm not searching for a man while unprepared to be a wife
Unprepared to be a mother, unprepared to be a lover
Unprepared to be the one whom you lay with under the covers

My main focus in life,
Is to be a faithful Christian
Doing the Will of God and living by Christ's mission

And no, I'm not conceited,
But that man will be blessed
And it's not because of the size of my butt nor my breast
But mainly because of prudence;

Conducting myself with wisdom
Baby girl possess more elegance than any euphemism

You'll never hear your homeboys say my name in the streets...
I'm a lady, I have never spread these legs between your sheets

Save the stereotypes, because I'm not that other woman
I'm not Mary, but this poem can show you a storm is coming

I'm not a gold digger
I'm not a whore, nor a slut...I'm not your shawty
And no, you cannot slap me on the butt

You cannot hit this and quit this; use this and abuse this
I promise, you'll be blessed
If you're seriously trying to choose this

I'm here today not because of the good that I've done
But, by God's Grace and Mercy...I was able to overcome
Physical and Spiritual beauty you can see
So blessed be the man who finds a woman like me

BEAUTIFUL THICK SISTA

BEAUTIFUL THICK SISTA,

I love the way you walk,

Your style, the way you ride...

The language of beauty when you talk

Holding nothing behind the bars of the cage inside of your mind

Speaking what you've been thinking,

And not waiting for the right time

BEAUTIFUL THICK SISTA,

I love the way you glide

Your stride has confidence...

The boldness in your eyes

Men are stricken by the beauty that you possess,

In spite of the scars that you've obtained...

From this prolonged fight for peace, joy, and happiness

Many blessings to all the **THICK SISTAS**

Who refuse to become just another behind kisser

Thin may be in, but **THICK** means you're rich

With all the characteristics of what it means to be legit

BEAUTIFUL THICK SISTA,

This one is just for you

Thin sin may sound fine,

But its beauty isn't true

BEAUTIFUL THICK SISTA,

I love who you are

The radiance that radiates...

From the largest of the stars

BEAUTIFUL THICK SISTA,

Keep your head held high

Heaven is your name...

Because your limit is the sky

MY SISTER

You're truly something special,
Just thought that you should know
I know sometimes it slips your mind,
Because you're always on the go

But, slow it down a minute,
And think about your worth
You get so caught up in helping the world,
That you forget to love yourself first

You're as beautiful as a rose
You're as lovely as a jewel
The old distress is over
Time for rebirth and renewal

Your heart knows how to love,
And when to cry out loud
You're truly a special woman,
You're **A SISTER** who makes me proud

STRIPES

STRIPES across a surface,

Kind of feeling like I'm worthless

Society has determined that this is really what my worth is

Feeling like a prisoner, **STRIPES** across my uniform

Born to be imprisoned, no beauty as a unicorn

STRIPED like a zebra, never to be a leader

My future has been determined,

Just another forgotten creature

But, my **STRIPES** represent so much more...

Than you would know

Not a sleep with me in secrecy,

Because you're keeping me on the low type show

These **STRIPES** are here for...

All of the times that I set up at night

Crying to my mother, because the Lord didn't make me right

He didn't conceal my **STRIPES**

I wear these **STRIPES** on my arm like pearls,

But it's funny how I can never see them...

On any of the beautiful girls

I'm not beautiful,

That's what you have told me

You turned me down before you took the time to know me

Too blind to see that my **STRIPES** were given to me...

By my insecurity

That you created as you consistently lowered my self-esteem

By saying, "You should look like this!"

Or "You should look like that!"

Or "Baby, you'd be beautiful if you weren't so fat!"

Or "Damn, I would never date a girl with a shape like that!"

These **STRIPES** are here for the babies that I've carried,

And miscarried from the stress I'm forced to carry

As you look at me after nine months of carrying your child

Burying me in tears...

Instead of lifting me in smiles

You have taken your own brush,
And painted **STRIPES** across my body
Creating an abstract painting, as if this was your hobby

When you were done, you wouldn't even acknowledge it
Fixed your eyes to look at me, like I wasn't fit

You've sketched this pain, these tears, and this hurt
But, you failed to sign your name on your own artwork

So as I scuffle to find the artist behind the painting titled
"STRIPES"
I'll continue to sign the anonymous artist formally known as
"LIFE"

WHO I AM

Should my neighborhood arbitrate where I'm headed in life?
Am I weak for possessing things I've regretted in life?

Do you ever look at me and think that I don't belong?
Who are you to judge me whenever I'm wrong?

Am I to be depressed, because I've never been rich?
Am I a prime suspect because I roll with a clique?

Do you ridicule me because of what I don't know?
Will you quickly turn me down, because I'm from the ghetto?

Do you think my only quality is running my mouth?
Am I bound to be a slave, because I was raised in the South?

Do you see me prison bound

Not later

But sooner

Because neither of my parents owned a High School Diploma?

Am I to be embarrassed, because I'm letting you know
the things that other people would rather keep on the low?
I really don't think so?

I could care less about your remarks,
The skeletons in my closet are drug out from the dark

Shedding light on my life is the only way for me to grow
I was once a young rookie, but I'm maturing into a pro

If you didn't know...
Here's your chance to find out,
That this is WHO I AM and this is what I'm about

If you don't like my lifestyle, then too bad for yourself
Because I love WHO I AM and I cherish myself

I'M TRYING TO DO ME

Just because I'm not 5'5 with hazel brown eyes
It doesn't mean I'm not beautiful,
You better realize

Because I'm not the model chic,
With a thin waist with thick hips
It doesn't mean you shouldn't show interest
To what proceed from my lips

Because I'm not shaped like a Coca Cola bottle,
It doesn't mean I'm not equivalent to America's Top Model

Once I look into your eyes and examine your soul
You will react like a letter and wait to be unfold

The love that I withhold is bold and often powerful
So don't front me off and set your mind to be doubtful

Unless you're unsure about yourself and not me
Because I was never blind...
From the womb, I could see

I know what's bothering you,
I can see the picture clearly
I can tell from the way you react...
That you fear me

I see the way you act when you're around the fellows
You watch me; you hate me, only because you're jealous
You wish you had a way with words the way that I spit game
I'm poetic, I'm powerful, and poetry is my name

Poetry is the game with such individuality
Never one in the same so respect that principality

So if you reverse every word that I said,
You would know not to judge the book cover...
Before you've read

This is a lesson to you haters always wanting to be
I'm not trying to do you...
I'M TRYING TO DO ME

THE PRICE

Is it all fine and dandy...
That you open up your mouth,
And discuss what's in my panties?

Undressing me with your eyes
Hovering over me like a cheap consolation prize
Wanting the peninsula surrounded by my thighs
When you're not even man enough to look me in the eyes

So what type of woman do you take me to be?
The do something strange for a piece of change, type freak?
Step into my world and take a front row seat

Because every night of the week, I fall down on my knees
But, your dirty thoughts have already placed me

At a place where society has placed you
You may not like the words I speak, but you will respect me
Because deep inside you know that what I'm saying is true

When I fall upon my knees, I pray for you and I pray for me
I pray for us and I pray for we, I pray for this society

Forty-five percent of women have been abused
Thirty percent remain confused
Twenty percent have been repeatedly used
And only five percent are standing in clean shoes

Self-respect starts at this very moment
This is your life so take the responsibility to own it

Don't let society live your life
Because in the end,
Your soul is **THE ULTIMATE PRICE**

INDEPENDENT

I'm an intelligent young woman with intellectual abilities
Flow so icy that I initiate brain freeze
If I speak into your ears
I'm guaranteed to make your brain freeze

My pictures are imperfect
But you'd still be willing to frame me
Ask yourself, "Could you blame me?"

Talent so explosive that I leave my pen flaming
Wild with my style, so name a human who could tame me
Altered my way of thinking
But deep inside it's still the same me

God is **number one,** and only He knows how He changed me
Used to be the type to react if you would name me
Opened up my mouth and yelled until my lungs became free
You know that it's plain to see

Search the world on land and sea
I bet you'll never discover another female who is just like me
Worry free and stress free

Always low key...
I'll never look to another to complete me
Because I operate **INDEPENDENTLY**

I'm the plainest Jane in the room, and I still stand out
Other women try too hard
I nonchalantly stand out

Not too proud, but I don't need a man to render a handout
I handle business like a woman
Therefore, you should know what I'm about

I have dated the thuggish type,
Who was always in the streets and kept me up all night

Even dated the type with the intellectuality,
He was garbage at the mouth, so I dumped his personality

I've dated the hard worker with the money on his mind,
Too busy for a woman, so I gave him to his grind

Enough of the lecture, so take it up with this gesture
Ladies...Get it together!
Weather out the storm and men will respect you
To the young and immature

Feeling as though they're grown
Check the last three letters and call me when you get your own

I excel by myself and it's no coincident
I'm not suffering for anything...
Because I'm **INDEPENDENT**

CAPTURE THE MOMENT

When I close my eyes,
I'm **CAPTURED BY THAT MOMENT** in my life

The **MOMENT** when I felt like somebody
Even though there were times in my life when I felt like nobody

Just as I had suspected it to be, no one was there
Everyone spoke with concern, but **no one** really cared

That **MOMENT** which I speak of was nothing like the rest
Physically I was my weakest, but mentally I was my best

I often hear the phrase, *"There is calm before the storm."*
And even the years know that months...
Are cool before they are warm

Before I tell the story of a **MOMENT** that seemed like forever,
I shall show you how things were shattered,
Before God put them back together

Before I saw the rainbow that dazzled within the sky
I longed to feel the rain, so I could understand why

Before I saw the stars that sparkled with such a glow
I desired to see the darkness, now I confidently know

If you would only listen to the words that I give,
You would understand that every flower dies...Before it lives

I died to all of my pain,
To live forever in all joy
Lessons learned and positive thinking,
Combined like an alloy

Everything that died within me,
Was used as fertilizer
A rose has grown that's more beautiful, than any other desires

Every day that I gaze into the mirror
I see beauty

There were days when I thought...
That I could **never CAPTURE SUCH A MOMENT**

But every day that I awake
I smile and give thanks to God
For allowing me to **CAPTURE SUCH A MOMENT**

THE EMBRACE OF BEAUTY

I **EMBRACE** what's rightfully mine
This body, these hips, these breasts, this behind
Beauty is a seed
Planted in the mind

To be fine is an understatement
Please don't waste my time
Valued over dimes
I'm one of a kind

A hundred dollar bill
Step to the light and check the line

Everything about me shows authenticity
Negative remarks only show simplicity

The world has placed a stamp on what's normal
Please open a dictionary and give me the definition of normal

People often fear what they cannot understand
So should I fear that there could possibly be a weight requirement to getting a man?

Do you think you'll catch a disease from shaking my hand?
Are you ashamed so you front me as a one-night stand?

Well, I won't stand for that demeaning type of action
Place me anywhere and I'm the main attraction
Once I show myself-esteem it's like a chain reaction
Women step above the line like the top of a fraction

I explain to them the definition of beauty
I save them from deceit
I feel that it is my duty

Truly, I believe that a woman can be
Anything in this world that she desires to be
Beauty is the description of a personality
So when I step to the mirror
I SEE BEAUTY IN ME

I COULD NEVER DENY THE FACT

As a little girl growing up,
I felt so odd in my ways
A little girl who never knew...
That there would be brighter days

No one would've guessed I had suicidal tendencies
Contemplated killing myself,
But God gave me a remedy

I thought that I was ugly,
but there was a storm coming
After the storm was over,
I saw the beautiful woman

You live and you learn,
But without knowledge you will burn
Knowledge paired with application a true prize will be earned

Look within yourself and come into grips with who you are
To you I may be nothing,
But in my eyes...I'm a star

I'm aware that I was formed from the dirt of this Earth
But, you can't tell me that God didn't have...
A purpose for my birth

If I'm anything more than you've expected me to be
Blame God for deciding to have FAVOR on me

I COULD NEVER DENY THE FACT that...
I'm indebted to Christ

And **I COULD NEVER DENY THE FACT** that...
I owe Him my life

I KNOW WHAT LOVE IS

Do I really **KNOW WHAT LOVE IS?**
Do I really know what it's worth?
Do I really know what I'm doing?

Showing you all of the belongings in my heart
Such as insecurities, impurities, and even expressing times...
When I'm not even sure of me

Hoping that this would be the cure of me
Turns out it's my disease; weak within my knees
I fall like leaves from a decaying tree

My soul is so windy and cloudy
Therefore, I cover up my feelings
Afraid to let you know about me
Believing that you would hurt me

I'm so deeply into me, that this body doesn't deserve me
Thinking it's only I who truly loves me
Because it was I who remained, when everyone left me lonely

Thinking that it was only I who stood by my side
Contemplating ingesting pills in an attempt for suicide

Thinking that it's only I who condense this cruel reality
By the words that encourages me to fall upon my knees

I constantly beg the Lord to deliver me...
From this Spirit of Caring
Whether a man likes what I am wearing

Or whether he thinks I'm cute, according to how my hair is
I'm confused...I don't know if it's too much to even share this
Because I love me so much...
That I would have an outer body experience

Strap a bomb to my waist and eliminate this ignorance
Just to save myself from these habits that are contagious
I'm the only cure to this disease that's so contagious

I must FIRST LOVE GOD and then love myself
Before I take on the challenge of loving someone else
I want to love my love until there's no love left
I want to overdose on my love and love myself to death

If I don't become an addict of my own love pills
Then I know within my heart that no one else will

DIFFERENT

Everybody has their own perception of life

What it is

What it should be

Nobody wants to agree

Everybody's claiming to be **DIFFERENT**

But, the underlying fact remains that everyone's the same

Same clothes, same hair, same house, same car

Even the same language

Leaving this nation tainted

With paintings of fainted artist

Whose exhaustion has led to death

Screaming for change

Begging the world to fall out of line with this ongoing routine

Put on by wanna-be thugs and destined whores

And I

Yes, I

Write lines like,

Wake up

Don't you want for more?

I can't believe the way that we fall to our knees
And worship everything EXCEPT God
And the world thinks that they've accomplished something
DIFFERENT

ALL LIES
They sound and look like everyone else
So I
Yes, I
Declare the title ***DIFFERENT*** because I'm nothing like you

MAKING ME HAPPY

I'm slowly learning how beautiful I really am

The road to survival wasn't the easiest

I've been through the storm and the rain

I've picked up the pieces of a shattered heart

Overall, I've felt the pain

I finally know how to live life

Mistakes come and go just as people do

But, I will always have to be the one to whom

I have to answer to

So as long as I'm breathing

I'm looking out for me

I'm doing what **MAKES ME HAPPY**

Even if it means dismissing people from my life

LOVE FOR ME

I want a **love** beyond measures

One filled with guilty pleasures

Hidden deeply inside the crevices of life like buried treasures

One filled with energy

A **love** that's deeply into me

A **love** so attractive that it draws even my enemy

I want this **love** to trace me like an outline

Tap me like a phone line

Lie on my skin for hours

As if, it changed its name to Calvin Kline

Top of the line

Love is at the top of my mind

Love applied for

At the bottom is where I'll sign

Love is often imitated by wet dreams and damaged sheets

But don't impose any of that knock off love upon me

There's only one **LOVE FOR ME**

So I refuse to settle for this lust found in the streets

The **love** that I speak of is that undying **LOVE FOR ME**

Entry IV: The Faded Story

(Then)

Dear Diary,

    Last night I was raped. I admit that I was somewhere that I should not have been among people whom I should not have been around, but that does not change the fact that no man has the right to violate me in such a way. My so-called friend witnessed everything. She even cried with me. When the smoke cleared, she told everyone she knew that I lied. My rapist was my ex-boyfriend, but we had never had sex. I never thought that he would stoop this low. I guess I just should have chosen my friends wisely. Diary, right now all I want to do is die.

Sincerely,

Ardreana

Entry IV: The Faded Story
(Now)

Dear Diary,

 Rape can strip a woman of all of her dignity. Then, she has to be nurtured back to the point where she can love herself again. For some women, this may seem impossible, but with God, all things are possible. If I can love myself again, everyone who has gone through such tragedy can do the same. Diary, right now all I want to do is live.

Sincerely,

Ardreana

THE FADED STORY

I looked into the sky and saw...

The faded glory

I looked over my life and saw...

THE FADED STORY

After the calm was over, I witnessed the raging storm

The lightning, the thunder, the danger that was born

The battle, the war, declaring what I had won

The pain, the cry, the sigh behind the moan

Intelligent, kind, beautiful, but still alone

When I was a little girl around the age of six

I knew of nothing more than playing mud pies and sticks

He said it was a game and tried to plant a kiss

But I quickly pushed away and asked,

"What type of game is this?"

He touched me where he shouldn't have

Therefore, I quickly ran away

I hid inside of my room and never again wanted to play

I said my prayers that night and cried myself to sleep
If mother would've known,
She would've killed him in his sleep

When I was a little girl around the age of eight
Walking home from the bus stop
I almost got raped

He grabbed me, he caught me
I screamed to my Savior
God answer prayers...
Because I was saved by a neighbor

As I rested on my pillow, I cried myself to sleep
If mother would've known,
She would've killed him in his sleep

When I was a little girl around the age of nine
The way the boys forced their hands between my legs...
That wasn't fine

My objection didn't matter because their hands were too strong
And I begged them for days to leave me alone

At a very young age, I learned to be tough
Just imagine how it feels when enough is enough

For weeks, even months, I cried myself to sleep
If mother would've known,
She would've killed them in their sleep

When I was a little girl around the age of thirteen
I met the first boy who lowered my self-esteem

He told me I was pretty, he told me I was fine
But when the school bell rang
I noticed he wasn't mine

For years after that, I cried myself to sleep
If mother would've known,
She would've killed him in his sleep

When I was a young lady around the age of fifteen
I learned to focus on myself and gained back my self-esteem

I fell in love with the girl whom I had known my whole life
If I could, I would make that young woman my wife

I fell in love with every single one of her qualities
If you haven't guessed it yet...
That young woman was me

As I rested on my pillow
I smiled my way to sleep
Mother had raised a woman
So, she took her final sleep

When I was a young woman around the age of nineteen
I met the young man who promised me everything

He worked and labored swiftly with tricks up his sleeves
But, he lied to himself when he thought I was naïve
He knew that I was ripening this fruit like brandy
So, he did everything he could to try and get in my panties

When I resisted him, he concluded our segment
By showing me that he could easily get another girl pregnant

I was hurt beyond measures and didn't know what to do
A million things may change in life,
But one thing remains true

God was there by my side every step of the way
No paths were visible, but He provided a way

There were very many nights that I cried myself to sleep
If mother was alive, she wouldn't have been able to sleep

When I was a young woman only two months later
I met a young man in whom I found much favor

He taught me to accept myself only for me
But, he made me feel that we were never destined to be

He let go of my hand, and pushed me into the cold
Literally leaving me without a hand to hold

For months, I cried frozen tears as I slept
If my mother was alive, she would've also wept

When I was a young woman around the age of twenty
I met the young man who offered to give me plenty

Blinded by false love, I gave him everything I could
But apparently, I couldn't give him...
What he thought that I should

He cheated, schemed, used, and lied
I prayed, labored, failed, and cried

Days upon days, I cried myself to sleep
I wish mother could help me bare the pain, planted so deep

When I was a young woman around the age of twenty-one
I lost my only sister and declared that I was done

I drifted away from God, and no longer desired life
I laid Christianity aside, because I was tired of this life

I wrecked my life altogether in a head on collision
When I chose within myself to make a foolish decision
I was under pressure and was surrounded by tension
Wanting someone to love me with the proper attention

He told me he cared and he seemed to have understood
But the things that are bad for you, will often look good

I became his fool and placed my heart in his hands
Heartbroken from the news...
That this was a married man

The hurt, the shame, the humility was my fate
By the time I lost my virginity...
It was a moment too late

Many days after, I cried myself to sleep
If mother was alive, this would've caused her to weep

Somewhere down the line only three months away
The worst day of my life took place, as I lay

If there's a day in my life that I'll ever regret
It's the day that this monster and I ever met

If I had known a couple of drinks would demolish my life
I would've never took the risk and made a roll of the dice

He showed his hate for me as he shot like a sonic
Wouldn't even stop the rape as I soaked in my vomit
I didn't show up to give my body to him
I was there because his cousin was my so-called friend

If it was a set up, I guess I never will know
But, I guess for even him, this was an ultimate low

He slandered my name and made me look like a harlot
My story, my life, contains deep stains of scarlet

I then became numb and walked away from everything
Depressed, torn, scarred, I had lost everything

I cried wide awake, I cried fast asleep
I found within myself the desire to die in my sleep

Mother couldn't help me, sister wasn't there
As I looked all around I found no one who cared

I was treated like a criminal although I was the victim
They praised him as a rapist and condemned me as a victim

Imagine having a million people look you in the face
And believe within their hearts that you're a total disgrace
Imagine being distressed and mentally displaced
Imagine having to stare your rapist square in the face

If it wasn't for those who love me, I wouldn't even love myself
They never gave up on me, although I gave up on myself

I thank God for friends and family too
If it wasn't for God, I wouldn't be speaking to you

I rose, stood, fought, and won
Was scarred, bruised, but defeated by none

So, I looked into the sky and saw...
The faded glory
I looked over my life and revealed...

THE FADED STORY

It all has been revealed, so who must I resent
Nothing and no one because the Lord is my strength

I once made the vow to never become a wife
Because a woman goes through hell, as a man lives his life

I pulled myself together and searched thoroughly within
And mustered up the strength to not harbor hate for men

Think before you hurt us and think before you act
Because we came from your rib
And not the lower side of your back!

MISERY

Where does it all lead?
Life that is

When I'm winning...
Why does it feel like I'm losing?

I'm constantly choosing between fake friends and imitation kin
Trying to figure out when all of the bull will end

I'm lost in a world...
Where being real about my feelings
Makes me less than a girl

But I'm a woman...Not trying to hide anything
I'm filled with shortcomings,
And things from the past that are not so becoming

I'm not a role model
I'm just being me
Because I don't believe in playing roles for this cinema
Called society

I can't be sold...
So stop trying to buy me
You'll never appreciate any of my efforts to give you
What's inside of me

Why be so focused on me
I never claimed to be perfect
I make mistakes everyday
So does that mean that I'm worthless?

When I curse this pedestal that you have put me on...
Am I wrong?

If I'm angry, why shouldn't I elevate my tone?
I shouldn't have to urge anyone to leave me alone

Alone is where I dry my eyes
I get teary eyed each time I displease the Lord
By leaving His principles behind

Alone is where I am,
With this pen in my hand
Dealing with the hurt of being...
Hurt by a man

Alone is where I reside,

With only Jesus by my side

Alone is where I'll be on the day that I die...

Alone I cry

So why taint the situation

By pursuing me like a degree and submitting your dissertation

About me

QUESTION:

Are you really that lonely...

That you'll do anything to get me to entertain the thoughts that are being formed on me?

APOLOGETIC?

Don't be...

Because there's one thing I understand

Sought after **MISERY** is always found by a...

MISERABLE MAN

IF ONLY

IF ONLY,

I could've known that this would've happened to me

There is at least one thing I would've done differently

IF ONLY,

I had used my head I would've never left the house

The choice I made was foolish and that's said without a doubt

How could I have been so stupid to put myself in this situation?

The Devil had plans for me, and so I fell into temptation

IF ONLY,

I had never gone to such a place

IF ONLY,

I would've stayed home

I never would've gotten raped

IF ONLY,

I had never touched that alcohol

I would've continued standing 5'4

Instead of feeling 3 inches tall

IF ONLY,

I would've known that I would've passed out on that couch

IF ONLY,

I would've taken heed to what those individuals were about

IF ONLY,

I would've known that this would've happened to me

IF ONLY,

I wouldn't have woken up...

But died inside of my sleep

Since God truly takes care of those He loves,

Woe to my enemies

Vengeance belongs within His hands

For whatever was done to me

It doesn't matter how many witnesses lied

Or what others may think of me

If God is for me,

Then not even rape can begin to bury me

As I walked passed those who knew...
They turned aside their nose
If I would've known they'd think I was lying
I would've kept my mouth closed

What really did it profit me to ask anyone for help?
If tears could drown a person,
I would've cried myself to death

I no longer say **IF ONLY**,
Because all is said and done
My life was filled with doubts and fears
And now, I'm down to none

What have I to doubt and who have I to fear?
At the end of every stormy day
A rainbow vividly appears

God is the most that I possess and the most I'll ever need
No matter what life may throw my way
I'll continue to succeed

SHE SCREAMS

SHE SCREAMS but she can't breathe

She's pushed out but doesn't leave

Cries for help but her tears on the market never release

Her beauty covers a beast

Perspiration starts to release

Sweat trickles down her forehead and pauses at both cheeks

You stare at her

Looking at her sweat you finally notice

Your reflection through her eyes and the look on your face is

Bogus

Surprise

Hocus Pocus

View me as John if you should focus

Because my beauty is my honey and my pain is my locust

I have no remorse or respect

For people who claim to love God

But see me dying and choose to stand on my neck

You are not what you claim to be
Mankind's worst enemy
It's a shame that you're not even half of the things
That you pretend to be

Because of you, a million boys and girls suffer rejection
Condemning everyone else and stealing from the collection
In my eyes, you are nothing
God is my protection

And Hell will freeze over,
Before you make me despise my reflection

I'm not saying that your entire life will be perfectly presented
But if you claim to be a Christian, make sure your heart is in it

There's no sense in pretending
That so-called Christians don't slander people
It's a shame how we carry on and call ourselves leaders

I was raped...
But it was you, who made me feel like a whore
You ridiculed me but encouraged him to do more

You smiled in my face and talked behind my back
Formulated your own story from some fabricated facts

I suffered panic attacks from everything that was done
I was in and out of counseling, while he was out having fun

But I know there is a God
And you can bet, He's looking down on me
It's He who brought me back to the woman, I used to be

I will not let this alter who I was raised to be
I was caged inside of my mind,
But God gave me the master key

How could a person of such a nature stand before a crowd
And sing like an angel, smiling with no frowns

And then build the nerves
To publicly state the words
"Yes I did it, and that trick got what she deserved."

Your scars are ugly
You will always disgust me
And regardless of what you think
I will always be lovely

ROAD TRIP

I hopped in my car and decided to take a **ROAD TRIP**
Not knowing that the wheels on my ride...
Would make the **ROAD TRIP**

They were tripping and spinning, spinning and tripping
As I was kicking and yelling, yelling and kicking
It was flipping and turning, turning and flipping
As I thought *Damn,*
"That officer should have written me a ticket."

Because I was driving way too fast for this traffic
Blood on the pavement, and now it all seems tragic
Who would've known the end of me would create,
So much havoc
If I would've known that this would be the finale,
You could've had it

So as I lay there, lifeless on the pavement
I still don't understand how you not know
What the word save meant
So many people could've saved my life
I'm not Jesus but sometimes I feel as though I gave my life

To a circle of individuals who didn't deserve it
And now I'm feeling that none of it was really worth it

At times I wish my mother would have gotten an abortion
Because when it rains, it storms and pours like Morton

Sometimes I feel like I'm on a saltbox
That little girl must be drowning out there on the saltbox

And it's been raining since before I could remember
For every single day from January to December

And the night that I knew it had rained the worst,
Was the night that the coroner had called the hearse

It was a head on collision
Done purposely by your ride
You killed me in an undying attempt for suicide
You murdered me
But you remained alive

I was dead and there was nothing to be done about it
No one was truly sad
It was only a competition of who could cry the loudest

I begged you to stop but you didn't
You stood there with those defying eyes,
Feeding lies to the world...
As I became the lawyer,
Presenting my case to a room filled with Judges
Trying to prove to them that I'm really not a bad girl

Therefore, they tripped and fell for your story
But, deep inside I know that you feel stripped of your glory

I waited on your table,
But, you refused to leave the tip
You should be proud for ruining my **ROAD TRIP**

THE LETTER OF A SCARED YOUNG WOMAN

Dear Lord,

Please forgive me for my many shortcomings
I am what I am
A struggling young woman
I pray that You accept me
For the woman that I have grown to be

I know that I'm not worthy of the breath You've given to me
I hate the company of others and I know that shouldn't be
But, I would rather just be alone
Because only You are a true Friend to me

Many pretend to be real with me and never fail to turn up fake
I've been through so much hurt
That I don't know how much more I can take

I love myself dearly, but I've grown to hate this life
The one thing that I desire is for You to take this life
Deeply within my heart, I long to be by Your side
I'm blessed to have Your love, but I often desire to die

Sometimes I wish that I were blind

Nevertheless, troubles forced me to see

I often wish that I were deaf

And couldn't hear the things said about me

I pray that you end my life at the next expected year

It would bring me joy if I could be taken away from here

        Sincerely,

        A Scarred Young Woman

TIRED OF LIVING

What is one to do when they've grown,

TIRED OF LIVING?

No longer driven to be among those...

With a need to be forgiven

Vanished friends

Useless family

All things seem so damaging

I close my eyes

Praying that God would close my file

Please Lord, please

Just eliminate my trials

And help me cope with being me

I'm thinking back to those who hated me

For whatever reason found

Woman down...

I'm damn near death

I suppose you're happy now

Up and down like an EKG
Fighting to open my eyes wide enough to see

Flat lined on the kitchen floor
Isn't that where you wanted me to be?

Slit wrist...Bullet to cranium
Pain planted like a geranium
In another element as if, I'm neck to neck with titanium

I'm tired...Do you hear me? I'm tired
I'm not sleep deprived, no victim of insomnia
I'm mentally delayed, emotions ruptured like a hernia

Please tell me what you are calling for...
Money? I have no more

The counselor has closed her door
Advice? I have no more

It's too late
My blood is already spilled along the floor
I can't take this anymore

So, I ignore your attempts to tell me how much I mean to you

There is nothing that you can do

I'm closed in like a cubicle

This stage isn't juvenile

So, I would appreciate if you not show up at my funeral

I'll be dead by then

And there'll be no more precious giving

You should have been my help

Before I grew **TIRED OF LIVING**

AM I?

When you look at me, what do you see?
Do you only see the one who would give it to you for free?

Why do you conclude such things about me?
Is it because of what your judgment have conceived me to be?

I'm guessing you assumed that I'd be less than a lady
Being aware that the average young woman
Have numerous babies

If I wear makeup and extensions in my hair
AM I the one with whom a married man would have an affair?

Did you take my kindness to be quite ridiculous?
Does my smile obviously mean that I am very promiscuous?

You seem to be concerned about the number of boys that I date
Paying no mind to the fact that I suffered a rape

AM I a slut because I made the worst mistake of my life?
Gave myself to a man and later learned of his wife

Tell me I'm a slut because I made bad decisions
Tell me I'm a slut and not worthy to be a Christian

Was I granted breast, thighs, hips and a butt
To be viewed in your eyes as a promiscuous slut

Take some thought of yourself and place no judgment on me
Because I only answer to the things
God has promised that I would be

FINDING A WAY

"I fold" is what they say when playing a game of poker
"Please hold" is what they say before the wait is over
"Man down" are the words when someone has shot a soldier
But when I awoke and smelled the coffee
It didn't smell like Folgers

At a loss for words
This isn't what I deserve
If life is grand
Tell me why it insists on destroying my nerves

Total anguish
Epic fail
To hit the head of the nail
But I am not a failure simply because my plan failed

So at the peak of the day
There has to be another way
And I'll find it
But I just wish that it could have been found today

MISUNDERSTOOD

Consider this...

No consideration from an inconsiderate generation

Taken for granted,

But the blame is from the seed that's been planted

Sometimes I wonder if I really belong on this planet

Angry?

How could I be?

Disappointed?

Why should I be?

Blinded by false minds

With your vision, how could you see?

I couldn't see the picture

Or maybe I just failed to have understood

I don't get it

I'm supposed to understand you

But I'm permanently **MISUNDERSTOOD**

MEMORIES

MEMORIES of who I used to be

Epiphanies of who I'm supposed to be

A reflection in the mirror

The woman...She looks like me

But she's not who I used to be

Or who I'll one day become

She's my addiction...That's why my veins are numb

I can't leave her in the mirror

Just to aim for something better

I said I wouldn't forget who I am

And I ended it with a never

Although she hindered me...I still loved her

She punched me emotionally...I still hugged her

She convinced me that I was nothing...

Until spreading my legs under covers

The same one who said it was fine to be depressed

About my mother

The woman in the mirror loved depression
So I fell in love with it too...She loved sadness
And somehow that expression...
Became glued to my face...Sad case

That woman is the woman that I never thought to replace
Until I realized that, she was the reason...
That I was losing the race

So I erased her
Finally found myself
Then I replaced her

I looked back into the mirror
I found the strength to face her

I cried...But I let her leave
She was my past,
Now I believe

I trusted God to make me whole again
Yes, I've been redeemed

BEYOND RECOGNITION
(In My Trying Days)

I can't recognize myself

I'm certainly not the same

All fingers pointed outward

Because I'm certainly not the blame

Cigarette smoke...Insomnia

But still strength lies in my veins

Your eyes can see my flaws,

But pupils fall blind to my pain

It rains on sunny days,

Inside of a lonely soul is where I reside

Finally aware that so many were only tagging along for the ride

In the midst of a negative surprise

At the break of my surmise

Somewhere the spirit speaks

And states, "This is how a fool becomes wise."

So many foolish plays

In all of my foolish ways

I now walk the path of sunshine
From my foolish choices made

I gave to so many; hoping to accomplish plenty
Love, hope, and compassion
Poured out my heart until it became flimsy
I never knew I had so many enemies

And still I wonder why?
Never knew that I...
Was provoking you to the point where...
You would make me want to die

So I cry and smile simultaneously
Because confusion is within myself
So many reasons to live
But still, I lie at the feet of death

So young is what they yelled
Pitiful is what it spelled
A rose held to your nostrils
But only blood, was what you smelled

"Help me" was what I screamed at night
Not wanting to exhaust the fight

Climbing through the bobbed wires of faith
Praying to God with all of my might

A veteran is what I am
Because I never gave up at war
Imprisoned in life's chambers
But, I never gave in to bars

Now here I stand so boldly
I'm strong in all of my ways
And I'm here to tell the story of all of...
MY TRYING DAYS

Entry V: Finally - Job 1:21 "The Lord gave, and the Lord has taken away; blessed be the name of the Lord."

Dear Diary,

    As you know, I have been through so much in my life. I have lost so many things that were dear to me. I lost my mom at sixteen, my only sister at twenty-one, and the only place that I could ever truly call home to a house fire.

    When I moved away, I faced more hardships than you could ever imagine. Not many people know this but there were nights that I slept in my car because there was no place for me to go. Diary, I was so scared. I have cried so many nights, but through it all, the Lord took care of me.

    I believe I stopped trusting in the Lord when my sister passed away. That was a very difficult time for me. The most hurtful part about the whole situation is the fact that so many people judged me instead of lifting a finger to help me.

    During this time of my life, I ended up losing my virginity to a married man. Had I known that he was married, I never would have touched him. The moment that I found out this devastating fact, I had lost a part of me that I can never again get back. I immediately repented of that sin and chose to remain celibate until marriage. I did my best to get back on track with God, but I was still a bit weak. The devil found a foot hole and ran with it.

My friends were the ones who drugged me down. On the night that I was raped, I was with my so-called friends. After the rape, they scandalized my name just to make themselves look good. Never did they think about how all of this affected me. I nearly lost my mind, but thank God, I didn't.

They are the very reason that I don't have many friends to this day. I can count on one hand the number of friends that I have. I'm not stuck up; I just choose not to fit in. When you stand out, you create your own destiny.

Although so much was taken from me, I gained more than you can ever imagine. The Lord has blessed me with strength, grace, and mercy. I will never try to make myself out to be more holy than Christ is because I know that I have made mistakes in my life. I don't practice doing evil, but sometimes evil follows me. Whenever it follows me, I pray that God strengthens me to resist it.

I am not ashamed of the things that I have been through because I am not still trapped in those things. Every day, I pray that the story behind my life can help some struggling young woman with the story behind her life.

Sincerely,
Ardreana

THINGS THAT ONLY CAME ONCE

Crying a million tears wouldn't matter

Because dwelling in the past...

Only makes today sadder

Looking into the future, only brings about anxiety

Trampling over the next man...

Just to come up in society

I wish that I could say the past doesn't exist

Then I wouldn't have a mother or a sister to miss

I guess that makes me mad at the world for not understanding

That asking me to just get over things...

Is a bit too demanding

Sympathy is a weakness, but grieving is a healer

Expressing is a deliverer...

But bottling emotions is a killer

I've lost every physical thing that was important to me

Now I'm imprisoned in a world...

Where I long to be free

Blinded from the tears and now I can't even see
Wishing to vanish away...
Into a land beyond the sea

I've lost things in my life that can't be bought out with gold
Things that have affected me emotionally and tarnished my soul

Sometimes I wish that I could burn into ashes beneath the sun
Because I can never get back...
Those **THINGS THAT ONLY CAME ONCE**

Somewhere in another life, I'll be joyous someday
That's why I often dream of Heaven...
When I kneel down to pray

LOSING MOTHER

If you've NEVER **lost** someone...
How could you tell me not to cry?
If you've NEVER healed...
How could you wipe my weeping eye?

Even though life goes on,
I'm still stuck in a phase
Visualizing you, but it's only within a daze

I keep begging for a cure, but all I'm receiving is pain
I keep begging God for sunshine,
But all I'm getting is rain

And still He took away the most important thing I ever knew
And now, I'm stuck on stupid trying to figure what I should do

Does God not love me like the rest of His children?
Does He not know my mother's love was one in a million?

Is this to reveal whether or not I am strong?
Am I selfish for thinking that God is doing me wrong?

Don't look at me and think...
How could she not have faith in God?

BECAUSE I DO HAVE FAITH

I'm not saying that I hate God,
Because I realize that God is the reason,
I'm breathing
But why did he choose to put my mother into ceaseless sleeping

Lying in my bed weeping,
Trying to make the tears decline
Trying to find a way to turn back the hands of time

And if time *could* rewind,
Would I want my mother here?
To suffer the way she did
And to watch it year after year?

So don't tell me not to express my emotions the way I do
Because the things that I write...
Are the things that I've been through

If you can't relate don't try to comprehend
Because I've seen numerous people...
Fake and pretend

To sympathize with the pain that remains within my heart
And the pain that I feel is tearing my life apart

So God please grant more mercy on my life
Because I'm emotionally bleeding...
From these slits in my life

PICTURE THIS

PICTURE THIS being the realest story ever told
My nephew lost his mother, at five years old

And I've experienced a lot of things tragic
But imagine being a baby, looking over in a casket

How do I make him understand...
That his mother is in a better place?
When his mother was set in stone,
At his final look upon her face

That's a tough case for anyone to embellish
So, I set my problems aside to care for his, not being selfish
I'm trying to teach him what death is
But, I'm failing on my methods

And now I know the true meaning of what...
A God sent test is
Some people swear that they are the best
When they haven't gone through the serious
This child has seen enough to make...
His whole world delirious

He has officially played his part in knowing what real pain is
He has felt the lightning strike,
So please tell me what the rain is

I've watched him cry many days and beg for his mother
And it irritates me like mosquitoes in the summer

So when guys come with drama...
I just tell them to their face
This is my child and they can never ever manage take his place

PICTURE THIS being the realest story ever told
My niece lost her mother at fifteen years old

And I've experienced a lot of things tragic
But imagine being a teen, looking over in the casket
I know she understands that she'll never get her mother back
Constantly feeling like...
She's being trampled on a train track

So I tell my friends to fall back,
I let her know that I have her back
Because I know that losing your mother
Can often feel like a heart attack

She cries, she screams, she yells her lungs out
Wishing her mom could hear the words...
Exiting from her mouth

"Mother, please come back, mother, it's a dream.
Mother why did you leave when I needed you here with me?"

But mother can't return,
And only God can heal the pain
I've experienced the same thing, and it can make you go insane

If you could only **PICTURE** the real stories of this world
Then maybe you'd live life as if you cared about this world

EMOTIONAL QUESTIONS

Mother, can you hear me?
Do you hear me mother?
Are you listening to my cry for you?

I'm screaming, but you won't listen
What's wrong?
What did I do?

Was it because I didn't do something you asked me to do?
Why are you ignoring me?

Do you not see the outpour of water streaming down my face
as I stand before this mirror?

I'm hoping that you would show up in this reflection of my face
But I can't see you through all of these tears
I guess it's because you had no fears

Well, if you did, I never saw them
Because I never saw you cry
But why mother? Why?
Why did you have to go off and die?

To some I may sound a bit outlandish
Way too old to not understand this

Handicapped by emotions that often demand this
There's an overwhelming feeling upon this soul
That's been damaged

Mother, why?
Why did you leave me?
Why did you get sick?
Why do you have me at the point where
I'm afraid to have kids?

I can't imagine my kids being left here,
The same way that I was left by you
In case you haven't heard...
Yes, it's true
Your first born did the same as you

Following in your footsteps,
Leaving my niece and nephew
And now they ask the same questions that I asked...
Mother, did you not know that I loved you?

Because if you did,
You would have never left me

I often wonder what I can do to make you come back
But I know for a fact
I have no control over that

So I avoid being angry at God
Just to be angry at you
Because maybe then
He'll allow me the opportunity to be...
Reunited with you

A MOTHERLESS CHILD

You don't know how it feels for paper to be...
The only one who you can talk to

Overtime,
I've learned that the only two who understands me
Are God and my notebook

Wishing that I had a living mother to express my hardships to
I can't even think straight,
At times, I can't breathe...
Some nights I don't even sleep

I'd be lying if I said I don't look up to the sky and cry,
Pretending that the stars hold the face of my mother
But there's no voice to accompany that image
No touch to add a brilliant finish

And people think I'm weird,
Because I spend endless days by myself
Just longing for one voice to call and say,
"Are you OK?"

But instead they say,
"She's acting funny."
Or "She's in one of her moods."

And if they do call...
They only want me to ignore my problems and focus on theirs'
They're all too weak to help me deal
With my nightmares

But I've been strong for others for too long
So tonight, I just want to spend time with my Lord...
My paper and my music

Because they're the only ones who understands the thoughts of
A MOTHERLESS CHILD

For once, I just want to dismiss the issues of everyone else
It's time for me to let others carry their own burdens,
By themselves

I've been spending all of my time trying to help
Children cope with missing their mom
Ignoring the tears of my own

May sound selfish,
But in reality I'm just like you
Selfish
I'm tired

There's no more for me to give to this undying world
Why not pull the plug, just so that I can live

The load is too heavy
I'm not Jesus
I tried to be like Him
But at this point
I'm tired of imitating Him
I just want to rely on Him

May sound crazy
And some may say that I'm just lazy
But I am only human

And that's why sometimes I avoid writing about my mother
An attempt to avoid reminding myself of the hurt
Of being **A MOTHERLESS CHILD**

YOU WON'T LET ME CRY

I wish I had the keys to unlock the bars...

That harbor my pain

But, I don't,

And since I don't...The tears remain

The tears behind my eyelids are ready to burst at any moment...

Like a bomb...

The flow is steady...

Leaving me to wonder when will my relief come

I know that you have the thought that only God can dry them

And I know that He will....

But He just haven't yet

And because He dries them,

It doesn't mean they won't come back

I know that they will come back, because I have a memory

This may sound stupid to you...

But, I wish that I could trade my day for yesterday

So that I can make my way back to my mother

I just want to let her know that I still love her

Sometimes I feel like I'm lying on a dozen knives
Or burning in unquenchable fire
Or even buried alive

I'm asking the question, "Why?"
I know they say I shouldn't question God

But, how else will I get the answer
The pain feels like a cancer

Where is my smile?
Behind these four walls,
There isn't one
Thoughts blow me into pieces like a loaded gun

Where are the happy thoughts and memories?
There are none without her

You don't know the pain, like I know the pain
You don't feel the rain, like I feel the rain

There is nothing else that I can do
But wear my pain inside out, just to please you

Because you don't feel comfortable seeing me sad
You don't want to see me cry
So, I just pretend that its second nature
To see another loved one die

But, when will someone other than me
Possess enough respect for me to say,
"Cry child, cry!"

And during the streaming of my tears, actually stand there
And help to dry my eyes
Knowing that this is a part of my strength and not my weakness
I'm flawed because...
YOU WON'T LET ME CRY

SET YOUR HEART ON HEAVEN

I know today is hard
I'm sorry for your loss
On Earth, the way to **HEAVEN**
Seems such a terrible cost

And though we all must go,
None of us want to leave
No family wants to be a part of the bereaved

When God calls a loved one home
Just think of things like this...
HEAVEN is our ultimate goal
Our Hope, our Prayer, and our Wish

So let your loved one walk the road that leads,
To the **Pearly Gates**

Yes, we're human
Of course, we'll cry...
But do not urge them to wait

Miss them dearly with all of your heart
But only for the space they filled

And remember that...
We all must die someday.
So **SET YOUR HEART ON HEAVEN** as you live

THE GREATNESS OF THE LORD

Philosophically speaking,
I was philosophically sinking
Into a deep sea that left hatred,
Constantly leaking

I'm bleeding, but all I feel is joy all around me
You say you found the Lord
Guess what?
The Lord found me

I was the one who was lost and sold out at all cost
Working without pay for one hell of a boss

Mr. Satan himself,
There is a wage called death
Had I continued following him...
I would have killed my own self

I write my stories on the pages of life,
So that you can see
But I'll fight until I can't, before I allow sin to bury me
My freedom wasn't free

Jesus Christ died for me; a propitiation, a price
Therefore, I fall upon my knees
I'm thankful and I'm grateful

You could never understand
THE GREATNESS OF THE LORD
Until it falls into your hands

THE OBJECTIVE IS TO FINISH

The hall is long, so I see that I'm in for the long haul
Walking pass doors and graffiti filled walls

No keys to be released, as I fall to my knees
If I can't walk, I'll crawl until my knee caps bleed

Alone but not alone, Spirits from the past haunt me
Memories of failed successes and fallen stands taunt me
Voices in my head speak firm voiced and bluntly
It split my personality more than Mother Nature does monthly

I've climbed the highest trees,
But I'm not to be compared to a monkey
I'm Black for a reason
The sun burns us in this country

The sun burns the physical, but people burn emotions
The love of money
Yes, evil earns a person's devotion

But no matter how much hell I sample before the end
It will never be pleasing enough for me to want to enter in
So as I walk down this hall

The sign reads *Life* at the entrance
They say that life is short
But to me it gets longer by the distance

If I never rest my head or never rest my feet,
It's OK because the only failure known is self-defeat

But I will never quit
I will never stop
I will never forget that God is MY ROCK

At the end...
When the exit sign flash before my eyes
I'll know that I have ran a good race

It won't matter whether I place first or last
Or whether I ran slowly or fast

It won't matter because...
THE ONLY OBJECTIVE WAS TO FINISH
And at the end of every race lies mercy on a blemish

DOWN TO THE GROUND

The rocks know me on a first name basis
At some point and time in life, they became my best friends
The hard surface built a foundation for me
It woke me up even when I didn't want to be awakened

Sounds funny but the pain pulled me away from my sleep
Making me uncomfortable with the state that I was in
It pulled blood from my wounds
And tears from my lacrimal glands

I screamed, "I give up! I quit!"
And out of exhaustion, the rocks cried out,
"Fine, stay here you're welcomed to lie on me
for the rest of your life. See if I'll help you again."

So then, silence arose
The rocks stopped talking
I had no more friends at the bottom
The ground would no longer comfort me
Because I had reneged on my part

So I cried

Day in and day out, I cried

Like rain, my tears poured across the ground

And finally, I couldn't cry anymore

The sun shined, but I wasn't satisfied

And then the ground shook

A rose burst through the platform of the Earth

It was I

I had taken root

A simple seed such as myself

I had become the prize of the garden

And that's when the ground spoke again

But this time, only through memory

I spoke back without failures' dialogue

I said, "Thank you ground

For working with me in my most unworkable moments.

Thank you God for rocks

For beneath them lies a beginning

For by them I have become a rose

I have overcome the ground."

THE ULTIMATE GIFT

I'm not worthy of asking that You save me
Although it's quite the thought
I'm only asking that You help me to worship You
Instead of these material things I bought

Not claiming to be religious,
But I would love to help the world
I'm only asking that You restore the joy,
That I had as a little girl

Not trying to quote the Bible
Don't want to know it all
I just want You to be there to pick me up,
If I should fall

Although I want my prayers to be answered
I know that there are certain things You'll keep from me
But in all of Your keepings,
Please dear Lord...
Freely give me all of my needs

Not asking to be a millionaire or the slightest form of rich
I just pray that when good and bad approach
You'll help me to recognize which is which

I love You with all of my heart
Though I'll never be good enough
Jesus, You are **THE ULTIMATE GIFT**
And Your **everlasting love** is a plus

PURE LIFE

Purer than life is what the bottle read that contained the water
That was clearer than crystal
Voices sounded off inside of my head like a fully loaded pistol

Nothing blissful about this story,
Still searching for the glory
Tried to pursue happiness in life,
But that was in a different category

So, the pureness from the bottle was a lying deceiving model
Tears burst before my pupils,
Speed at full throttle

Nothing about this life is **pure**
All I've seen is filth
Taught to follow wives' tales and mammy made myths

Nothing I've seen has been clear enough
To give me a straight answer
All I've seen are emotional parasites
That eats away at the soul like cancer

People prancing before God with their man made religions
Forcing the whole nation to cling to man's decision

I'm not married to your opinion
Nor am I under your dominion
And I'm definitely not basing facts on a scientific dissension

I don't trust a soul on Earth
Because I know that a bed of Satan's lies
Lie and rest upon this Earth

My faith lies in God and not a soul alive can change that
I love because of Him
My thoughts and feelings of Him remain intact

Jesus is the only **PURE LIFE** that I will ever know
His blessings shower like drops of rain on the field,
Where Spirits glow

But sometimes this life gets lonely,
Because I can't see the God on high
So I think back to that bottle that read ***PURE LIFE***
And I smile my way through the cry

THE PERFECT MARRIAGE

I fell in love over time
Couldn't think of anything else
Couldn't think of anyone else

He had my heart
He raised me
I was weak, He made me strong

I was low, He was my high
They knocked me down to the ground
So beautifully, He lifted me beyond the sky

This Guy...Like no other
Wasn't the ordinary lover

Protected me like a father
Nurtured me like a mother
He let me cry on His shoulder like a sister
Gave me advice about the world like a brother

When you called me a slut...A no good screw up
He was the one who said proudly, "I still love her."

He knows me...Everything
He stands close to me through everything
I'm married to Him happily
I don't have to even wear a ring

Because our love is not defined by things that look fine
No amount of money could express the way,
He has become mine

He belongs to me...I belong to Him
Strayed away a couple of times,
But I'm lost without Him

To Have, to Hold, to Honor, and to Cherish
Nothing in this world could make me want to leave
THIS MARRIAGE

I've never been so happy in my entire life,
Until I married my Lord and Savior, Jesus Christ

IN SPITE OF ME

You loved me when I was unlovable

Wrapped Your arms around me,

When I wasn't huggable

Carried me to a resting place, when I was weak

When I had walked a thousand miles,

You healed my feet

I'm indebted to You, but the bills remain outstanding

I'm confused as to why,

You would help a soul so demanding

I was a mess up

I fess up

I'll never try to dress it up

I messed up so many blessings,

Thinking that I wasn't blessed enough

Greedy was my mentality

I'm grateful that You put up with me

So selfish that at one point,

I actually thought You were my enemy

Filled with contaminants
My inner soul was so filthy
But still, You loved me
You've been more than a friend to me

I would kiss the ground You walk on
Even though I'm not worthy
Would scream Your name to the world,
Even though I'm not deserving

I LOVE YOU,
But those three words
Would never be enough to contain You
No simple emotion would ever be enough to obtain You

You're picture perfect
A glass square could never frame You
Who dare love someone like me?

Yes, I blame You...I'm thankful to be alive
My heart is open wide
Longing for Your presence
Please let me bow before You come inside

Although my voice isn't fit
For You I will sing
And for You I'll give my life
Because I owe it to You as my King

~FINAL THOUGHTS~

I like to believe that the skies cry for me
The clouds droop low as the sky slowly turns gray
Heavenly eyes in the sky leak drops of water
That resembles my tears

But, why are the skies crying for me?

My sad days are gone
And I surely don't need anyone feeling sorry for me

Midnight has come and gone
No more dark skies
The sun is bursting through the horizon

But wait!
There's a shower of tears pouring from those large white clouds

It makes no sense to me
The sky is the prettiest shade of blue,
But the clouds are crying

I finally get it...When the skies cry for me,
They cry tears of joy

THE CLASS OF 2007

Dedicated to the Class of 2007
At Wilcox Central High School (Graduation)

As I reminisce about the first time, we set foot into a class
I wonder how many people actually thought...
We wouldn't last

And even now, I often sit and think within the same
How many people thought that our diplomas were in vain?

Let me inform you that they will smile in your face
And hope for you to fail and end up in no place

This is reality and life is now a competition
The Class of 2007 is on a mission

To prove those people wrong who titled us as failures
So, we as the **Class of 07'** bonded together

We bonded, we grew, and we united as one
You probably never thought we'd be as outstanding as one
We never hesitated to tackle our goals as one

Now we will step into the future and face the cold as one
Thanks to all of those who believed in our goals
For helping us to travel every road that we chose

There are not enough dollars in this world to repay
The debt we have created as we have journeyed on our way

This is not the end for us,
But more of a strong beginning
For everything we lost,
We can now look forward to winning

We have made it this far through determination and dedication
Now we can thank God for granting us this graduation

PEN TWIN

Dedicated to my Pen Twin, Jameese K. Wright
Thanks for believing in my writings!

We finish each other's lines

As though we think with the same mind

God blessed us to be on the exact same path

Just in the nick of time

We stood in line

Wanting to be soldiers

We both fell

They ran us over

Lying flat on our faces

We provided each other closure

We were **TWINS**

Born from the same exact **PEN**

We were sisters,

And to me that meant we were more than just friends

When I fell, she picked me up

When they were shooting, I made sure she ducked

We both relied on blessings when the world relied on luck

When the world said I was nothing but a no good slut
She slit her wrist,
So that she could feel my pain through her cuts

When they stomped her to the ground
Kicked her when she was down
I fought for her
Injured them all with the biggest stick that could be found

She's **MY TWIN**
Born of the same ink
We live by the same words
And by the same brain we think

As I cried on her shoulder
She held my tears in her hand
Our sisterhood will never be determined
By a simple friendship band

When her eyes cried a river
I allowed it to flow into my heart
MY TWIN
The devil in Hell will never tear us apart

There aren't many people...
Whom I'm willing to call my friend
Thus, we bleed the same emotions
Through the **PEN**
She's **MY TWIN**

THE MAN OF GOD

This poem is dedicated to every man of God who has ever walked the face of this Earth, especially my dad. Thanks for teaching me the greatness of God.

God created man in the image of Himself
Therefore I know **The MAN OF GOD**
Is sho-nuff something else

Never mind the things you thought or the things you long to say
What God has planted in the heart of man
Shall withstand the trials of day

I'm here to tell you something that you may or may not know
The MAN OF GOD is here for God
And does not stand for a show

Tell me have you seen a man with faith like Daniel
Trapped inside of the Lion's Den
But knew what God could handle?

Have you not seen a man with mighty strength like David?
Faced with life's many giants
But through God,
Oh yes, he made it?

Tell me have you seen a sinner just like Saul
With a life so turned around...
That they had to rename him Paul?

A man of imperfection with qualities similar to Peter
But because he keeps on striving, he's fit to be a leader?

What about a man with patience such as Job?
In the midst of all of his troubles,
He still holds on to hope

A man who's just like Jonah, has been in the belly of a whale
A man who God has joyously found a temple,
In which he can dwell

A man who puts aside his life and exalts Jesus perfect story
Give honor where honor is due
BUT, GOD GETS ALL THE GLORY!

How do you say thank you,
To someone who helps you to understand God?
You encourage him to continue being that...
MIGHTY MAN OF GOD!

ABOUT THE AUTHOR

Ardreana Thompson was born on February 6, 1989 to Carl and Dora Thompson. She was raised in the small town of Camden, AL. At a very young age, her parents instilled in her the value of having a relationship with God by attending worship service every Sunday, except for illness.

The youngest of five brothers and one sister, Ardreana grew up very quickly. She spent most of her young life helping her sick mother as she underwent dialysis and chemotherapy. At the age of sixteen, Ardreana lost her mother to kidney failure and cancer.

In May of 2007, Ardreana graduated from Wilcox Central High School, Camden, AL at the age of eighteen. She was voted "Best Writer" of her class. Shortly after graduation, she went on to attend college at Faulkner University in Montgomery, AL where she majored in Elementary Education. With no knowledge of what the future held, Ardreana would soon be facing many obstacles.

In the spring of 2009, Ardreana's family lost their home to a house fire. In an effort to continue with college, she began working as a caregiver for a small daycare center. She then became a part-time student.

Living alone for the first time with only a minimum-wage job, finances became overwhelming. Ardreana eventually quit school and soon after became homeless. Church members gave her the help she needed to rise back to her feet. Then she decided to move to Orlando, Florida with an older brother. In search of a better life, Ardreana made an effort to make things work. Quickly realizing that the Florida life was not for her, she moved back to Alabama.

Shortly over three weeks after moving back to Alabama, Ardreana lost her only sister to sarcoidosis (a disease in which inflammation occurs in the lymph nodes, lungs, liver, eyes, skin, or other tissues). After the death of her sister, she grew distant from everyone except her niece and nephew. In an effort to help them as much as possible, she took a job at an automotive plant as an assembly worker. She later re-enrolled in school.

In September of 2010, tragedy was at its peak when Ardreana was raped by an ex-boyfriend. This event was so traumatic that she quit school for a second time and eventually lost her job due to an inability to focus. Ardreana soon drifted into a deep state of depression while clinging to sleeping pills as a method of coping with the pain. After nearly four months of caging herself in a closed bedroom, she finally reached out for help.

In January of 2011, Ardreana was hospitalized for five days due to the traumatic impact that had taken a toll on her life. During hospitalization, she was diagnosed with Post-Traumatic Stress Disorder. After nearly a year of therapy, Ardreana's life seemed to have taken a total turn around. She is a rape victims advocate and attending college full-time. Her past dreams of becoming a teacher have now changed to becoming a nurse. She now holds a special interest in a future of helping rape victims. Although her career plans have changed, she still harbors a unique love for God, helping others, children, and writing.

COMING SOON...

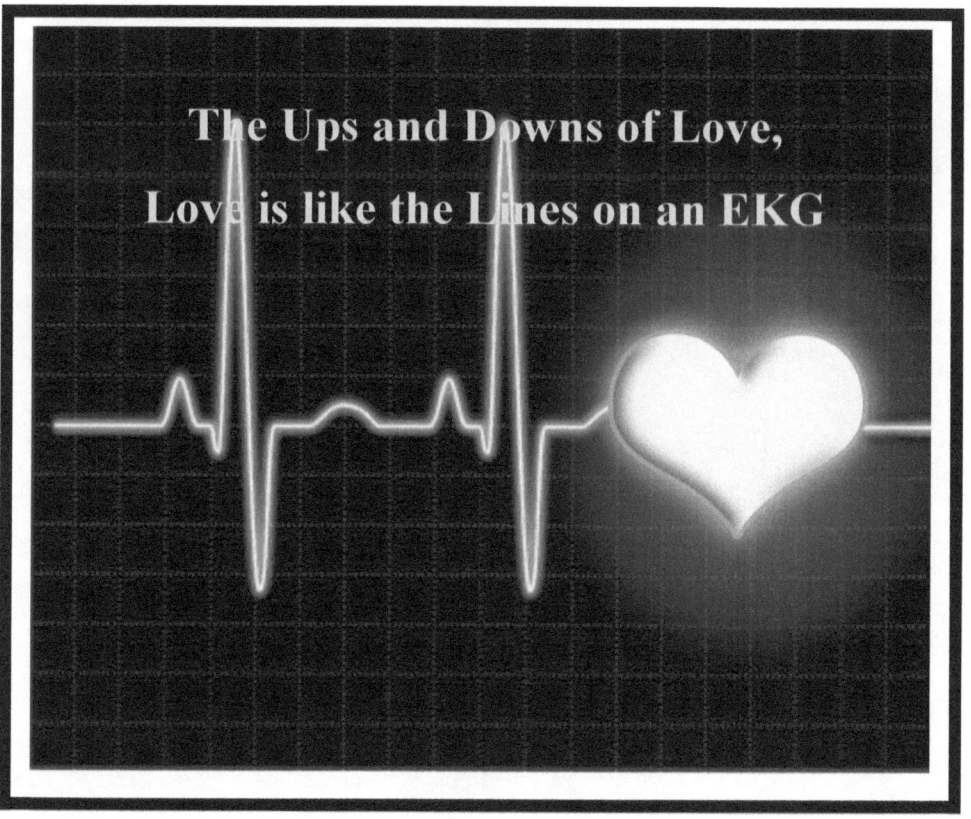

www.ingramcontent.com/pod-product-compliance
Lightning Source LLC
Chambersburg PA
CBHW031246290426
44109CB00012B/456